The

What happe1

child has a mysterious illness

(as told by a sibling)

Sharon S. Hogan

Contents

This book is dedicated

to my sister Eileen, my inspiration,

Dan, my first best friend,

and Tim, the keeper of all good memories

Know all the theories, master all the techniques, but as you touch a human soul be just another human soul.

- Carl G. Jung

Illustrations

Preface

There is a crucial and daunting question that I seek to answer:

I was engaged in volunteer work with an activist group in Cleveland, Ohio, registering voters in poor neighborhoods. Someone recommended we connect with an interfaith group, to help get more registration volunteers on the street. A meeting was set up; I assumed I would be telling their representative what my group was doing, what we knew about the targeted neighborhoods, and where we had found people in need of registration.

The young woman, that the interfaith group sent to talk to me, began by telling me at length about her personal experiences overseas with a religious organization that helped poor people. This was all friendly and fine, but I was interested in getting down to organizing our now larger pool of volunteers to register as many voters as possible. She then began asking me about my life and my childhood. I thought this was odd as I was middle-aged at the time and could not understand how my childhood related to the project we were supposed to be working on. But to satisfy her curiosity, I told her that I grew up in Connecticut and that my older sister was mentally disabled.

"Well," she asked, "How did growing up with a handicapped sister make your life different?" I thought for a moment and answered as honestly as I could, "I don't know. I have no idea what my life would have been like without her." The conversation became awkward after that: Would I be registering voters in poor neighborhoods if I didn't have a disabled sister? I thought, "Does this make me who I am? Who would I be if not for this experience?" Even though I have often wondered about it, I find such things hard to imagine. How would life have been different if I had a typical big sister to talk to, compete with, argue with, and share thoughts with? Would I have been happier? What would my family life have been like if I was an only child, or had only brothers? My imagination fails me each time the question arises.

What I *do* know is what it was like to have an older sister whose behavior and problems could not be defined or adequately described in the 1960s when we were children; or, in the 1970s when we were teens and then in our early-mid twenties. The disorder that plagued her was not even listed in the Diagnostic and Statistical Manual of Mental Disorders until 1980 (DSM III).

I am able to describe what it was like to growing up in the family I grew up in, and how my sister's mysterious illness affected me. However, I can't know how different it made me. I'm sure one result of my sister's disability was that I became more interested than most children in reading and thinking about psychology, mental illness, and what makes people tick. I don't know that I would have felt compelled to study psychology and make it my life's work if I not had her as a sister. I can't imagine what else I would have done with my life and I don't know what kind of person I might have become.

I've come to realize that there was something in addition to my sister's condition that gave me a peculiar role in my family. Being the most talkative child somehow made me more likely to be corrected and ridiculed. Rehashing anything silly or mistaken that I had ever said as a kid became a common pastime for my mother and father. This set the stage for my words to be mocked either as I was saying them, or flung back at me at a later time. My arguments would be dismissed without consideration and my experiences and feelings were usually discredited; in short, I was set up as the untrustworthy buffoon. Since I was not suffering from any apparent mental or physical maladies I was expected to tolerate this treatment without complaint. So, as the healthy and strong child it was my place to serve as comic relief. I was the source of funny material for everyone—including Dan my older Brother by one year—except Eileen who was not inclined to talk; and, my younger brother Tim, for as long as he was too young to participate in this dynamic. Later, he too joined in the fun. I learned that this behavior continued in my absence long after I had moved away and had my own family.

I am aware that as a human being I am subject to the biases and filters that affect memory. As humans, I think we are very good at recalling selective facts that support the conclusions we have already drawn. I seek patterns, make connections, and create correlations by focusing on evidence in favor of my view while ignoring evidence that refutes my view; this confirms my beliefs.

For example, I formed a negative impression of a young woman named Roxanne who had left her husband and daughter to have a Navy career. She had married and divorced twice by age twenty-seven. I was gossiping about her impending third marriage when Mary Lou, a friend, suggested that I reinterpret my view that Roxanne might be someone who tossed husbands aside when she found that they were no longer suitable. Mary Lou considered Roxanne as someone who had been unfortunate in falling for men who had let her down. Mary Lou had her own history of failed relationships. I had pegged Roxanne as a party girl, but my friend had seen a heart-broken young woman who had tried and failed at finding a good husband. We each recalled Roxanne's story through different lenses and then came to different conclusions. I realized that I might have been wrong about Roxanne.

I am likely to recall misunderstandings as the result of the poor communication skills on another person's part, rather than my own failure to pay close attention. These are the ways I filter my memories like most humans do; and, this is known as self-serving bias.

So: how would my life have been different without a disabled sister? This question remains in the junk-box of my memory. It rattles a bit more than some thoughts but keeps finding its way to the surface whenever I try to sort out other items from my past. I remember all sorts of things and I think and talk about those people, events, or places. I have read, studied, and taught community college students about how the brain works, how memories work, and how feelings and beliefs affect memories. I try to understand my life through the filter of my own perspective and know some of the tricks that the human brain can play on my memory and perception. I know I will tell my story in a different way than the people who shared some of my experiences might recall the same story. Each person recalls a personal version of reality with a different meaning, based on the particular filters of their mind.

In addition to this unanswerable question, there was one particular statement in my mind which was so overpowering that I dared not write my personal history until November, 2017. While I was growing up, and for many years after I became an adult, my mother would tell me, "If you ever write about your life, leave me out of it." This literally happened hundreds of times. I don't know if she said this because she disapproved of what I thought, because she disagreed with my views, or because she just didn't like the things that I said. "If you ever write about your life, leave me out of it," again and again and again.

There were plenty of times she insisted, to other people and to me, that I lied all the time. I'll admit that with her, sometimes I was consciously lying (Perhaps five percent of the time). This is an estimate based on my recollections but I think I was telling the truth more often than not. I believe what my mother was trying to tell me was, "I don't trust your point of view, and you shouldn't either. I am right, and you are wrong." She was often that way with other people too. It is clear also, that my mother expressed her anxiety about me writing about her when I wasn't there. She told people that she believed I would write about my life and hers someday. It was not, and never would have been, possible to write about my life and leave my mother out of it. I tried a few times to write in journals and diaries, but her repeated demands that I was not to write about her haunted me enough to prevent me from making any progress. Then she died.

FLOWERS

I like flowers

Just like you —

Spring may shower us all with flowers

Just like me.

I like flowers colorful

I like flowers just like you.

-Eileen

Chapter 1
The Fairy Child

Stroke

Ginny (my mother) was at home, winding down her Sunday activities in early November, 2017 when a blood vessel in her head exploded. It was Ginny's dream home—a spacious house in Waterford, Connecticut. She had designed it, decorated it to her taste, and lived there for thirty-five years. She and her husband, Jack (my father), had obtained a  large waterfront lot on the Niantic River. The area was still a sleepy suburb of New London. The Millstone Nuclear power plant had been completed in 1971 and expanded in 1974-75. There was a hydrogen explosion in 1977 that killed a worker. It was, and continues to be, the only Nuclear power plant in the state. That initially worried potential developers; but my parents still built the house there. The central portion of the house was modular, with a two-car garage and an attached passive solar south-facing greenhouse. This glassed-in southern addition radiated heat from the sunlight into the colonial home even on the coldest of winter days so long as the sun was shining. Electric baseboards supplemented the natural heating. Sea breezes from nearby Long Island Sound cooled the house and surrounding area during the summers.

People eventually calmed down about the nuclear power plant and several ostentatious homes were built nearby. Jack and Ginny's property met the river with a marsh and a small beach so they built a dock for boating and swimming. In the summer months they enjoyed evening cocktails on the beach before dinner. The house lay on the east side and the sunsets were spectacular over the water and lowlands on the other side of the bay. Ginny had surrounded the house with flowering gardens: variously colored peonies, lilies, other flowering plants, and shrubs in long broad beds bordering the neatly cut lawn. She started tomatoes and melons in the greenhouse that were destined for planting outside as the seasons progressed. Outside, the gardens bloomed and produced. Inside, the house was decorated with art, antiques, and items scavenged during many years of operating their real estate business. They dealt in all kinds of properties—buying, selling, and renovating for rental. On top of that, the lifetime of accumulated possessions from three generations of Ginny's and Jack's relatives found their inevitable way into the house as parents, aunts, and uncles all died. When Jack's older brother Bill (my paternal Uncle) died, his photo albums, WWII medals, and memorabilia were added to the archives.

Three months before that fateful Sunday in November, Jack had been moved to a nearby nursing home. Nearly ninety years-old, he had been suffering from dementia and other chronic ailments. In his last years he had a tendency to wander along the street or in someone else's yard, sometimes intending to join the Navy or go off on some other equally absurd quest. When he could no longer walk, he was taken to the hospital and from there to a nursing home. Ginny visited him daily, but he lasted only two months. He went from not walking to not speaking to not responding, to dying.

That Sunday, Ginny had been a widow for three weeks. She was adjusting to a life no longer burdened with the care of her husband. She now had only herself and one other person to look after: her sixty-two year-old daughter, Eileen (my older Sister). Eileen was unable to live independently and had always lived with her parents. Ginny was, at that point, just beginning to catch up with household work and the late autumn maintenance of her beloved gardens. She had shopped and even attended a memorial service for her sister-in-law on the afternoon of her stroke. She was still energetically shopping, cooking, and taking care of herself, her home, and her daughter. Her youngest son lived nearby. Tim (my younger Brother) was in his early fifties, and had been trying to help his mother through Jack's decline; however, she did not readily accept help. She liked to do things her way and she had difficulty relinquishing control.

Those who survive hemorrhagic strokes (a form of CVA [Cerebral Vascular Accident]) describe the head pain as sudden, intensely painful, and debilitating. That Sunday, Ginny's last act may have been to go to her desk and call for help. The office was in the corner of the open living area, where a door led to a short stairway down into an unheated room that connected the house with the garage. That room had served as an office for the family business when they had meetings and deals to make. It gradually came to serve only as the front entrance to the house and storage space for old files and furniture. Ginny may have fallen against the wall beside the door—or against the desk—before slumping to the floor so close to the door that it could not be opened.

Eileen wandered the house attending to her own needs, ever passive in slippers and a faded nightie covering her slight frame, She saw her eighty-five year-old mother on the floor and assumed that Ginny had decided to sleep on the worn out, orange carpeted floor. Eileen turned around and walked into the living room, over to the dark green couch where on any other night her mother would be dozing off. She then took a blanket off the couch and covered Ginny with it. Having taken care of her mother as best she could, Eileen went to bed. Never in six decades had Eileen been encouraged to answer the phone or, for that matter, taught to make a phone call. She had no inclination to communicate except when to make her own simple needs known. She had a second grader's level of literacy: if she ran out of cream for her coffee or instant coffee, she could write 'creem' or 'instint coffee' on the shopping list, but hardly much more. Ginny had not encouraged Eileen to develop skills that would make her more independent.

Ginny lay on the floor all night with a blood vessel spilling into her brain. That same night, Tim was on business in a neighboring state. He was usually in town, working at his used outboard motor repair-and-sales shop. Tim lived above the shop in a modest apartment, but he regularly ate dinner at the house—where he had lived well into adulthood. However, this weekend he was servicing a motor for a distant customer on Cape Cod. He had spent the night and then met with his customer on Monday morning. Tim called the house and tried to reach his mother. No one answered on either her cell phone or the land line. He knew Eileen was there, but she was not up to the task of any help. So he therefore called his shop.

The shop was only a fraction of a mile from his mother's house. Tim asked Devan, his office manager, if she would go to the house and check on his mother. When she arrived, Devan entered the front room and went up the short stairway to the main living area. She was unable to open the door because Ginny's body was blocking it. Unaware that there was an unlocked back door, she called Tim back. He quickly assessed that something was wrong if the front door could not be opened. He told Devan to call 911, and that she could enter through the back. Tim got into his truck and drove back to Waterford as fast as he could. Devan found Ginny on the floor under the blanket.

Paramedics arrived and took her to the hospital. That morning, I received a phone call from Tim. I saw his number and recognized his voice. He was on the highway, getting information relayed from Devan. His first words were, "Mom had a stroke." He briefed me on what he knew and I encouraged him to stay calm and drive carefully. I couldn't help in any way except to listen and offer support since I have lived six hundred miles from Waterford, Connecticut, for many years. Never regaining consciousness, Ginny died a week later.

Jack and Ginny Get Married

Ginny's father Albert (my maternal Grandfather) came from a family of Italian laborers who grew up in servant's quarters behind the estate of the Palmer Family who had made their fortune in the textiles industry. His father, Alberto (my maternal Great-Grandfather), tended the grounds of the estate. Albert met his wife Lily (my maternal Grandmother) at another estate where she served on the kitchen staff. It was the summer home of a New York "aristocrat." Lily had emigrated alone from Finland.

Based on high school yearbooks and photo albums, as well as reports from her friends, Ginny was a happy girl who was blessed with movie-star beauty. The family lived in a little house that once served as a bowling alley, complete with a tilted living room floor. Ginny was successful both in curricular and extracurricular activities at school. She belonged to all sorts of clubs. She had led the marching band as the drum majorette, was popular, and had many friends.

Ginny was possessed of a great sense of style and was skilled in the art of sewing. She fashioned much of her high school and college wardrobe herself. Some of her clothes were made from the fabric of an army surplus parachute that Albert had found. It was probably a nylon parachute because Japan was no longer selling silk to the US (This was the World War II period when Japan and the US were at war with one another). She could dye the fabric or leave it white to make silky blouses.

The technical high school she attended taught sewing and cooking skills to the girls, and mechanical crafts and woodworking to the boys. Ginny refined her sewing skills and also took college prep classes. Her excellent grades qualified her for a partial scholarship to Connecticut College, a small, private liberal arts school for women.

The high school yearbook indicated that Ginny hoped to become a fashion designer, but Albert would not endorse that dream. However, He would support her if she attended the local woman's college as a commuter and studied to become a teacher. He wanted her, if necessary, to be able to earn a decent living. Ginny liked languages, so she studied Spanish and became a certified high school teacher. She married soon after she graduated and did some substitute teaching before having children. Then she helped my father to start and run a number of businesses.

Albert had to defend his decision to his tradition-bound family members to provide for Ginny's college education. According to their view, beautiful women could marry well without the time and expense of an education. College was either for wealthy women who went to finishing school or for homely girls with little or no hope of finding husbands. Women, who weren't interested in husbands, or supporting themselves, could go to convents. Girls generally weren't considered worthy of education for their own employment, enjoyment, or ambition in those days.

When Ginny attended college, she worked during the summer selling ice cream at Ocean Beach Park in New London, Connecticut. Her uncle Gus (my maternal Great-Uncle) was the manager of this city-run resort. World War II was now over; the economy boomed, and soldiers and sailors returned home to buy houses and to attend college on the GI Bill. My grandfather believed education was important. He said, "Education is something nobody can take away from you." He had worked hard all of his life and many of the things that he had earned had been taken away from him. He had won a scholarship to college, but when the lady who ran his boarding house fed him only a lettuce sandwich for dinner each night, he nearly starved. He was a tall young man on the football team and had to return home to his family to get enough to eat. He later built a house and lost it, paying all of the medical bills when his wife became so sick with tuberculosis that she nearly died.

Ocean Beach Park had a long beautiful sandy beach, with amusement rides and a huge swimming pool. Some of the lifeguards doubled as exhibition divers who performed stunt diving shows for the summer crowds. My father Jack was one of those divers. He could bounce on the high diving board, do a flip and land on the board again and then flip a few more times before entering the water while barely making a splash. The stunt performers also did clown dives like belly flops and the "watermelon" (These dives produced maximum splash). Jack was a competitive diver at Boston University (BU). He graduated from BU with a degree in public relations.

Many families only supported higher education for male children in this era when women were often sent to college only to meet a suitable young man. It was where women could find the men who could achieve the status that even the smartest and most ambitious women were barred by custom and tradition from positions that paid well.

Ginny made it to graduation. Many of her classmates fell in love and dropped out to marry and support their husband's goals. Many dropped out to marry before their pregnancies became obvious, or failing to get a ring, they went away and sometimes gave birth to babies to be given up for adoption. Ginny beat the odds and graduated.

Ginny spent her senior year in a language immersion program in New Hampshire. This was the first time that she had lived away from her parents, and Jack visited her regularly from BU; eventually, they became secretly engaged. At this point in time, official engagements had to await parental permission and the man had to be in a position to provide for a family.

Jack already had a job lined up. He polished his shoes and dressed in a suit and tie in order to ask Albert for permission to marry Ginny. He spoke to his future father-in-law alone in the living room while Lily waited in the kitchen. He probably had to describe his job prospects and impress the older man with his suitability as a provider, husband, and likely father to future generations. Albert gave his blessing; he later admitted the shiny shoes had impressed him. Many poor boys had learned to spit-shine leather to a high gloss in the military.

When Jack exited the house through the kitchen, his future mother-in-law told him that if he had asked her the answer would have been no. Lily believed that at twenty-one, her daughter was too young and deserved to have some fun before settling down. Lily had emigrated to a foreign land alone at twenty-three and enjoyed living in New York for three years before her marriage to a younger, less worldly man. Ginny, in contrast, married an older, worldlier man. They were married in 1953.

Although Ginny was younger than her fiancée, and had only lived away from her parents for two semesters, she was the better student by far. While Jack had a quick wit, and many skills, he had to admit that in many ways Ginny was smarter than he was. He would complain (in a way that would later be known as "humble-bragging") that it was difficult to be married to a smart woman. They would be unconventional in agreeing that a wife could be as smart or smarter in some ways than a husband, but in all other ways they maintained traditional roles, including the division of labor of men's and women's work. Ginny graduated with a teaching certificate. Her college yearbook description indicated that she about to get married and that she had some psychic abilities.

My father's side of the family story in America begins in Ireland during the potato famine of the 1840s. People often ask me if I am related to someone else named Hogan. I reply, "Probably in the way that we are all related somehow but, if so, they are not my close relatives. There aren't very many of us." I was recently able to verify that my Great-Great-Grandparents did indeed come from Ireland in the mid-nineteenth century. They arrived on crowded ships during the 1840s and many got sick and died during the ocean crossing. Those who survived the passage faced discrimination and poverty upon arrival. They became laborers, dressmakers, and sign painters.

Compared to other immigrants, the Irish had some advantages in assimilating. While the Irish immigrants did experience cruelty, starvation, and discrimination, their pale skin, pronounceable names, and use of the English language allowed them into mainstream American more readily than the darker and more culturally-varied immigrants or former slaves.

When my son had to write about his ethnic identity as a homework assignment, he wanted to know "what made our ancestors come to the United States?" I thought about that and told him that everyone left their homeland because they had no reason to stay. No status, no property, no education, and in some cases no food. It took several generations for them to become middle-class Americans. The Italian and Finnish side would rise a bit more quickly than the Irish, but they came to this country later, and so were able to ride the wave of prosperity that industrialization brought. Jack would be the first in his family to go to college, and he was the only one of his family's generation to complete a four-year degree.

His brother Bill (my paternal Uncle) was eight years older than Jack. Eleanor—his sister (my maternal Aunt)—was four years older than him. Jack was only two when his father, Daniel S. Hogan (my paternal Grandfather), died. He could not remember him at all. Eleanor and Bill remember their father as having had a bad temper and they hid from him when he was angry. They refused to share this information with my generation until their mother, my maternal grandmother, Kathryn died.

Kathryn Hogan refused to talk about her late husband. When asked about him she would say things such as, "he's dead and doesn't matter." It may not have been a happy marriage. After Daniel died Kathryn moved on to a new life. She traveled around the state fitting people with medical corsets, which was a standard treatment in the 1920s and 1930s for both bad backs and gynecological problems. She primarily raised her children alone but she did have a lover for many years. He was a stepfather of a sort to Jack. He died when Jack was in his late teens; and, Kathryn sent Jack to his funeral. There Jack was stunned to find that this man, who had been like a father to him, had a wife and children who Jack had never met or even known about.

Kathryn had three mates: two husbands of her own, and one who was married to someone else. After losing her husband first and then her lover, she eventually married a widower named Oliver Plouffe. This was one year (1952) before my father and mother got married. I grew up calling Oliver grandpa, but Jack made it clear that Daniel Hogan was the name of his real father and the deceased boyfriend's name was forgotten, or suppressed, in the course of time.

Jack told me about his childhood. After his father Daniel died, his mother had to work. She put him in first grade in a Catholic school, because the public schools did not accept children until they turned five. Jack started first grade at age four. He was dyslexic. This trait appears in my brothers as well. When I learned to administer IQ (Intelligence Quotient) tests, I would see that they were very intelligent, but they had brains that were more adept at certain skills, but were not as good at other tasks. When Jack started school, dyslexia was just an esoteric idea very few people knew about. His teachers assumed he was unable or unwilling to read and write well. He would be punished and belittled for a condition that he had no control over. His ambition, creativity, and talents would go unnoticed in school. Jack spent four years in the first grade getting beaten by a nun because he couldn't read well enough.

It is possible he might also have been a bratty little boy. He was essentially being raised by Eleanor and Bill who were only children as well. He did learn to read eventually, slowly and haltingly, and struggled to learn to spell. Comic books helped him learn; and eventually, Kathryn hired a tutor for him.

Jack spent much of his youth at the local YMCA while his mother and older siblings worked. He learned how to play sports, develop acrobatic skills for stunts, and to swim; there too, he learned to dive. He studied drums and developed his ability to the point where he was able to work as a jazz musician and singer. Although raised by a single mother, he was not as deprived as many poor children. His family lived in cramped apartments but, despite that, photos and stories reveal they were not hungry and were able to afford good clothes. Jack had many toys, and there was music in the home. Jack had guidance and role models. Bill was a quiet and studious boy who left high school to help support the family by working as a machinist. Bill gave Jack toys and a drum set. Bill had a Victrola that played 78 RPM records. He also collected early jazz and blues singles.

When the war began, Eleanor became like *Rosie the Riveter* (the name referring to women working in the war industries at that time) and built submarines. After Pearl Harbor was bombed, Bill joined the Army Air Corps (The Air Force had not yet separated from the Army). Bill learned aerial gunnery (how to aim and fire .50 caliber machine guns), and became a tail gunner on B24 Bombers. He went off full of enthusiasm to help win WWII for the allies. Bill's plane was shot down over Germany, and when he landed—despite the parachute—his leg was broken. Captured, he was shipped to a prisoner-of-war camp (a Stalag—the German word for "prisoner-of-war" (POW) camp; it is a contraction of the German **Stammlag**er, which in turn is a contraction of a German polysyllabic three-word designation). Eventually, he was treated in a German hospital, where they re-broke his leg which had healed poorly. When he was able to walk he was sent to another Stalag. Yes, he was an actual *Hogan's Hero*. He watched the TV show of the same name, in which a group of international POWs outwit stupid Germans (ironically, played by Jewish actors). Bill asserted that the actual POW experience was not nearly so much fun as the TV show—which he loved anyway. He just barely survived World War II and when the war ended he carried only 110 pounds on his six-foot frame.

Jack was working in a machine shop after school when he found out Bill was reported missing. When he asked to go home to console his mother, his boss told him no: "We won't be able to beat the Germans and the Japs (this was, and remains, a common slur used towards the Japanese) if you take time off." While Bill was still a POW in Germany, Jack convinced Kathryn to permit him to enlist. So Jack dropped out of ninth grade (he was old enough to enlist because of being held back by his dyslexia), to join the war effort. Jack joined the Navy and went to gunnery school. He learned to take apart and maintain the large guns that could still be seen on the topside of Navy ships during my own armed service years. For the first time in his life, Jack was a good student. He began to consider himself intelligent. Ambition led him to take extra training, and exams in order to qualify to serve on submarines, and earn his GED. He always credited the Navy with making him the kind of person who could go to college and start his own business.

Social status differences and the strict segregation between officers and enlisted men inspired my father to go even further and pursue a college degree. Although he had not seen action in WWII, he benefitted from the GI Bill, and was able to attend college without going into debt. He would wear his college ring throughout his adult life. My parents wanted only two children. I was born in New London, Connecticut, in 1957. I was the third child and Ginny would remind me of this often as I grew up.

As an adult, I studied the history of birth control to understand why I came to be the third child in a family where only two were wanted. Birth control pills were not available until 1960, but in most of the United States, condoms and diaphragms could be used by anyone who wished to have sex while preventing children.

The Comstock laws (enacted in 1873) still outlawed birth control in Connecticut and Massachusetts when my parents were married. Not only The birth control pill, but any birth control device was deemed illegal. In 1965, the Supreme Court case declared these arcane laws unconstitutional—see *Griswold v. Connecticut*, 381 U.S. 479 (1965). The new law did not come quite soon enough, and so in June of 1966 I got a baby brother, Tim.

The Family Moves to Tariffville

In 1959, Jack got a new job at Combustion Engineering, a company that manufactured fuses for explosives. And so the family moved from Waterford, in the southeastern part of Connecticut, to Tariffville, a village northwest of Hartford, closer to the center of the state.

My earliest memories involve moving from that one home to the other. I remember the floors we played on. I have vague recollections of carpeting on the floors of the previous house. The floor was my world. As little children do, I crawled around, learned to walk, fell, and sat on the floor most of the time. There were three of us little children, and I was the youngest at age two, Danny was three, and Eileen was four. I adored them and enjoyed playing together with them on those floors. Eileen and Danny had been born a year and a week apart. My parents had tried to stop having children, but as it turns out, they were only able to slow down a little. I was born a year and three months after Danny.

I also remember the floor of the car. I must have been almost three feet tall at the time we moved, and could walk and talk at the time. The old house had smooth oatmeal-colored carpet. The new home had harvest-gold sculpted wall-to-wall carpet. I used to stand on the hump of the car where the drive shaft was housed and was able to peek over the back of the front seat. In contrast to the plush carpeting of our home, the back of the car had a gritty, scratchy rug on the floor and the drive shaft bump. It was a new ranch home in a development built in the 1950s. The development contained about one hundred-and-forty houses, with its lots perched on a hillside along the east side of the Farmington River valley. We lived on the western edge of the development on a street that was aptly named West Point Terrace. Our lot had a pronounced incline. The slope made it possible to walk in the front door on the east side of the house facing the road, then go downstairs to the basement level and step out into the backyard, which overlooked the valley.

We enjoyed a spectacular view of the river, and the hills—we referred to them as mountains—on the far side of the river valley which appeared blue. Light rays that carried yellow color faded out in the distance while the deep blue rays reached our eyes across the valley and we could view the sunset as it slowly descended behind those hills. The incline behind the house was too steep to build on. As the neighborhood filled with families, it became known to all of the nearby kids as Hogan's Hill. They came each winter with sleds and aluminum flying saucers to slide down our hill.

On chilly fall mornings the river valley filled with thick fog, while in the winter, a picture window in our living room would be covered with lovely fern-like patterns of frost. As the sun passed over the house and shone on that window in the afternoon, the frost melted and pooled on the window sill. A cat—one of a series—would sit below that sill, eagerly awaiting the moment when a silvery bit of water would drip down. The drop immediately soaked into the gold carpet and the cat would pounce on the wet area where the drop fell, appear confused and then shake the moisture off her paw. This could go on for hours. I could watch the cat for a while, but not for hours. I'd then find other things to do. Eileen liked cats, but what she loved was cat fur, on a live cat. She liked to hold a cat and place her forearms on their coat. Sometimes a cat would go along with this.

Things were good when the family moved to this house. Eileen was still developing normally. Danny at one-year younger was growing as well, but small for his age, and a bit timid. Ginny reported that he cried when he was introduced to the lawn on a warm spring day, and that rather than crawling and exploring this new kind of carpet he wouldn't move. On the other hand, the ever-resourceful Jack made many home improvements primarily with his own hands and hard work. One such project was constructing a thirty-three foot (ten-meter long) pool in the backyard. It would become an attraction for all of the kids in the neighborhood. There were many happy and splashy times in that pool.

Jack's new job at Combustion Engineering was solely in the personnel office. It was a step up from his job supervising the security department at Dow Chemical, where he had been working in personnel as well. He soon realized there was more money to be made by finding people with technical skills to work in these industries. Skilled engineers, scientists, and technicians were in short supply, and the companies that needed them paid hefty fees to those who sought out and found the employees they were looking for. Jack observed that small agencies—doing what was casually referred to as *headhunting*—were making more money than he was.

When Jack resigned to start his own business, his boss said, "You have a wife and three little kids, and you are going out on your own? Man, you have big balls!" Jack started his own employment business and became a headhunter. Ginny managed the office: she did the books, the typing, the filing, and answered the phone. Jack acted as head of sales and recruiting. They called their business Personnel Search Associates. Jack traveled around the country recruiting clients and marketing their skills to potential employers.

Ginny would sit behind an IBM *Selectric* typewriter in the basement—now paneled and filled with sleek office furniture—and run everything else. There was an extension phone upstairs in the kitchen so she could take care of business while doing housework or attending to us children. Wearing an elaborate bun or French twist hairstyle, she kept pencils and pens stuck in her hair. This made it convenient for her to jot down a phone message in the kitchen, or write down ideas anywhere in the house that she happened to be.

Things That Go Boom

The economic boom of the twentieth century came from a convergence of American natural resources (iron and coal), industrial development, and government spending on weaponry during war. Before the US entry into each World War, America was a significant source of munitions to its Allies. Regardless of the natural resources and the best efforts of the New Deal policies of the 1930s, it was only America's entry into WWII and the resultant War Command Economy (State Capitalism) that by the end of the War the US controlled half of the entire wealth—or capital—of the planet and was the superior military force.

The state of Connecticut was home to a large number of companies that supplied the War Department (renamed the Department of Defense after World War II). Electric Boat was a prime submarine manufacturer, employing engineers and union workers in the southeastern part of the state. The Colt firearms company was based in Hartford. The northwest suburb of Hartford was also home to Ensign Bickford Industries. These makers of explosives, plastic, missiles and all manner of innovative weapons like napalm (Dow Chemical), helped make Connecticut one of the wealthiest states in the country. After the war, money continued to flow in and the long-established businesses of Insurance and Finance still flourished.

Skilled workers without college educations could build submarines, guns, and bombs for first, WWs I and II, and the subsequent wars that the United States was involved in. They could earn good union wages and benefits. After WWII, the GI Bill would give millions of young men educational opportunities that enabled them to do very well. The Cold War escalated in 1947, shattering the fragile wartime alliance between the US and the Soviet Union. It required better missiles, bigger bombs, and lots of nuclear submarines.

Fear of rising communism and the power of the Soviet Union brought a fever of panic that came to be referred to as the Red Scare (Although a similar *Red Scare* had occurred post-WWI). This was a war of ideas that pitted western capitalist democracies against socialism, communism, and even atheism (and by extension, with the godless communists). The national motto was changed from *E Pluribus Unum* (Out of many come one) to *"In God We Trust."* The phrase *"under God"* was inserted into the previously secular Pledge of Allegiance.

Some believed that the Soviet Union was spreading communism throughout the world, one country at a time. It was up to us "good guys" to prevent additional countries from becoming communist, or soon they would fall one by one into communist-controlled, or spheres, of government; until, we would all be speaking Russian or Chinese (The Chinese Communists had assumed power in October, 1949). This fear was good for the "military-industrial complex" that then President Eisenhower later warned us about during his last speech as departing president in 1961.

In the 1950's, the United States assisted France monetarily (Two billion dollars in 1954) to hold the line against communism/nationalism in a little country called French Indochina. Its people called it Vietnam. The US got involved in preventing (What then Vice-President Richard Nixon would explain) the so-called domino effect. War was good for business in Connecticut.

Connecticut sits between the great cities of New York and Boston. While much of the state has remained rural since Colonial times, dotted with small towns and farms, along the coast and large rivers industry developed: fishing, whaling, liquor, and textile manufacturing. It was in a prime location for the eighteenth-century British shipping routes that flourished with the slave trade. British ships collected slaves in Africa, transporting them to the Caribbean Islands and Southern colonies. In Jamaica, Antigua or Barbados, slaves were sold. Sugar and molasses were purchased then loaded on board. In the American south, more slaves were sold, and cotton bales replaced the human cargo.

From there, ships headed north. In New England, cotton was sold to factories to be made into thread and fabric; molasses would be made into rum. Those finished products were loaded onto ships bound for Europe. Mills, distilleries, and factories created the jobs and cities that sprang up all along the navigable Connecticut rivers.

Tobacco fields were cultivated under tents of cheesecloth to protect the leaves from excess sun and wind. Those leaves were handpicked and carefully dried to make wrappers for fine cigars. In the south, leaves were exposed to sun and wind. The lower quality tobacco that came from the South, mostly Virginia and North Carolina, was made into cigarettes. Premium southern tobacco crops were sent north to become filler in expensive cigars wrapped with the more costly shade-grown Connecticut tobacco leaves. While cigarette smoke and ashtrays always seemed stinky and vile to me, the late summer smells of cultivated, fresh growing tobacco and harvest tobacco drying in ventilated barns were unforgettable fragrances when I grew up in northern Connecticut. In the summer, boys and girls at who were willing to work that kind of labor could make better than minimum wage in the tobacco fields.

Ramshackle buses traveled around our neighborhoods picking up kids as young as fourteen to spend their days working under tents in the tobacco fields. It was hot sweaty work, and those who did it absorbed nicotine through their skin and became addicted to it (or more addicted than they already were). Very few suburban kids did this kind of work. Southerners and Puerto Ricans were hired and housed in seedy camps that were hidden off back roads. They stayed for the season and after the harvest went back to wherever they called home.

My birthday in late March, 1957, placed me right at the peak of the Baby Boom. I was busy learning to crawl seven months later when a significant historical event took place:

Russia launched Sputnik. This little Russian satellite would cause a panic regarding the state of education in America. The Space Race escalated the Cold War. Money poured into public schools in an attempt to make the children of the Baby Boom (loosely defined as the period from early as 1943 until the last cutoff date, 1964) the best educated in the world. Baby Boom males older than me, born in 1955 or earlier, were drafted to fight a war in Vietnam, which we watched on television each evening as I grew up. Later in the evening, we would watch old movies and TV shows about WWII, portraying Americans as brave, heroic winners.

Eileen gets Sick

According to old home movies, reports from my parents, and my own earliest memories, Eileen was as well-adjusted as any child for the first few years. She smiled, toddled, laughed, talked, and had fun playing with others. Then at age four, something happened that made her very different. It started with an adverse reaction to a shot. It could have been any of the shots given in those days: diphtheria, whooping cough, tetanus or smallpox. She ran a high fever and cried all night. The fever broke, but a few days later she developed a painfully swollen ankle.

Eileen was taken to the doctor, who couldn't determine what her problem was. Other than her evident distress with the swelling and pain, Eileen still acted as you would expect a four-year-old to behave. She paid attention, answered questions, and followed directions. Next, she was sent to a specialist. The specialist put a big plaster cast on her leg and foot. At home, her ankle swelled further inside the cast. Her toes began to turn purple. She was taken back to the doctor.

By Ginny's account, the doctor had a terrible bedside manner. He told Eileen, "Hold still," while the child screamed. He yelled at a nurse or assistant to hold her down while she struggled in terror, confusion, and pain, and then he removed the cast with an electric saw.

Eileen was never the same again. From that point forward, she giggled for no apparent reason. She no longer communicated in words like she had been doing. Eileen would get uncontrollably giggly and shout "POO POO." She did not respond with fear when she was scolded or spanked. She talked in poetic nonsense.

I was two-and-a-half years-old at the time, but by all reports, I was a very talkative child. My brother Danny was very quiet. So I talked to him and I remember saying to him, "Eileen used to be good, but now she is bad." I remember him agreeing. The things that seemed bad to me were: she would repeat words and giggle hysterically; she would not stop when told, "that's enough;" nor was she responsive to any such demands from parents that usually work on small children. She didn't seem to care if she was being yelled at or told that what she was doing was wrong; and, she rarely cried.

It was as if she actually had entered another world and was not affected by things in our world. Sometimes she seemed frightened: She was easily startled and occasionally bothered by loud sounds so that she blocked her ears when jets passed overhead or trucks rumbled by. Sometimes she was amused and smiled a little at the antics of other kids; often though, she was racked with giggles over some secret. When asked what was so funny, she might repeat the word that she was amused by, or she might say, "Nothing!" She sometimes made up words or word associations. Once when the game "badminton" was mentioned, she said "naughty mitten" and giggled. She would repeat words she seemed to find interesting. She seemed to love the camera name "Polaroid" and would repeat it then giggle.

The Fairy Child

When I was little, I regarded Eileen with awe, the way younger children often view their older siblings. I liked it when people asked if we were twins or commented on how much we looked alike. I felt honored to be dressed in the same outfits for special occasions and to wear the clothes that she outgrew. There was a short period when all three of us—Eileen, Danny, and I—were very close in height. Occasionally, people asked if we were triplets.

It seemed to me, in retrospect, that Eileen was a changeling, a fairy child. This idea that some children are taken by the fairy folk and replaced with a fairy child was how pagans in the British Isles explained children who seem to be in another world From medieval times until the nineteenth century, there were stories about children and sometimes adults who had been switched with, or taken over by, fairies throughout northern Europe, England, and Ireland. It is likely this mythology was used to explain children who had various mental and physical health problems as well as Autism. When I was little, I sometimes entered fairyland with Eileen to play.

In the spring and summer, we would go out picking wildflowers. Eileen made up names for the flowers. We would gather the flowers in a hole in the ground. We called it a flower cave. Some decades later, it would become fashionable to arrange delicate little plants and miniature objects in pots or gardens and call them fairy gardens. Eileen and I were way ahead of that trend with our flower caves.

We saw Polaroid cameras advertised on TV. Eileen invented an outdoor game called *Polaroid Pigs*. In the summertime, she liked to chase my brother and me as well as the neighborhood kids around the front yard, yelling "Polaroid Pigs! Polaroid Pigs!" We played along by making grunting noises and crawling around under the juniper bushes.

Eileen could spend hours with crayons and paper, making abstract geometric designs. Once, she made a collage out of brown construction paper on a white background and brought it into the living room. "Look, kids, I made a POO POO," she said, giggling hysterically. This would have been funny if it wasn't so strange. She walked around the house and the yard, searching for imaginary friends. She would call out to someone or something named "Snowy," and could not find him, her, or it. She couldn't, or wouldn't, tell anyone who or what "Snowy" was, or why she was calling to it.

At this point I want to make something very clear: although Ginny would later express her frustration toward my teenage ways in a fashion I considered abusive, she was not abusive to, or neglectful of, her babies. She was warm and affectionate when we were little children. She may not have been perfect, but if her style of mothering could cause the extreme change in behavior we saw with my sister, why wasn't I likewise affected? She did not treat me, Danny or Eileen, any differently. If cold mothers, who are by no means rare, could switch healthy children into severely limited Autistics, there should have been many more children with the kind of problems Eileen was having. Eileen would not receive a proper diagnosis for her psychiatric problem for another thirty years. Experts believed bad mothering caused mental illness in children at the time that Eileen began acting oddly.

Eileen did not go to school when she was old enough to start kindergarten. Ginny kept her home for a year, which was allowed, and sent her to kindergarten with Danny. The accepted age at the time for starting was age five (reached before the first of the year). Eileen and Danny both had December birthdays. This made Eileen only slightly older than her classmates, but Danny was among the youngest. He had to repeat the first grade when he had difficulty learning the alphabet. I remember being very lonely and sad to be left home when I was the only one not old enough to go to school and I would miss them when they were gone.

Things did not go well for Eileen in school. She did not have the social sense kids usually pick up from observing others. She did not listen. She would throw things out of the windows. She took off her shoes and socks and washed her feet in the bathroom sink. When the other kids found out she was open to suggestion, they told her to do disorderly things. She didn't have the sense to say no.

Ginny drove my brother and sister and the girl up the street to school, taking turns carpooling with the other girl's mother. When Ginny chauffeured, I rode along. One day as the kids were let out of the car at school, I slipped out, went in and joined with them in the kindergarten classroom as though I belonged there. I was able to stay quite some time until they noticed me. Ginny got home to a ringing phone. The school was calling to report that she had forgotten me. She said that it was embarrassing.

Her not noticing of my absence on the return trip she explained as the result of having a very stressful day. On top of homemaker duties and minding me she was, after all, spending time in the basement helping to run the headhunting business while my father traveled. Although she was home like other mothers, able to watch us kids, cook, clean and chauffeur, the administration tasks of the business always awaited her. Perhaps my mother's forgetting me was symbolic. Her oldest child was a "special" child, and life was challenging. Life would have been less stressful if she could just forget about that third unplanned and unwanted child.

That first year that my older siblings went off to school, I was left to roam the living room while the easy listening station played Ferrante & Teicher piano duets— their arpeggios and flourishes—were worming their way into my brain with the very oxygen that I breathed. This kind of music would forever make me feel lonely and long for company or, at least, some sort of diverting toy or activity.

I remember how much I loved my big sister. As I got older, I tried to copy her unique artistic style, and how she would cover any scrap of paper or cardboard with geometric designs. She was the family artist. My own efforts at art showed some promise, but I rarely persisted in any medium. Eileen made art every day, any time, and from whatever material she found. She especially liked the boxes that butter came in. These boxes could be opened out flat, with various folds, flaps, and tabs that had locked it into box form without glue. Their unusual outline fit well with Eileen's uniquely colored creations.

While we were all still young children, Eileen would get silly and invent quirky games. Danny and I played along. Once while we were all on a bed, wrestling and tickling each other the way kids often do, Eileen began saying "meat feet."

She would then grab one of our feet. We played keep-a-way with our feet, while she grabbed at us, saying "meat feet" again and again. Danny stopped and asked her why she kept saying that. Eileen grabbed his foot and said "meat feet to eat!" then playfully bit his foot.

Autism I

Though research on Autism has increased dramatically in the last decades, there are still many unanswered questions. What did people think about an oddly withdrawn child before modern theories? British folklore had a suggestion: Fairies kidnapped the child and left behind a changeling. The changeling looked exactly like the kidnapped child but was an impostor. The human child was gone; the changeling would live among the humans, but in body only. The changeling-child's mind remained in the mystical land of fairies.

Perhaps this idea became popular because so many children looked human, but were far off, unreachable by their families. Changeling myths may suggest that Autism is not a modern disorder, but has been with humans for centuries

When Eileen was born in December of 1954, she was a perfectly healthy baby. After the dramatic events that so changed her behavior—at this time in history—only a few researchers were attempting to identify children with this disorder. There was no single term to label it, and there was very little agreement about how to describe or understand what caused it.

The history of Autism diagnosis is a story of slow steps, piecing together an understanding of the disorder, and distinguishing it from related mental disorders. However, it is also a story of misinformation. To illustrate how slowly the process of understanding progressed: the first two editions of the standard mental health reference work, *Diagnostic and Statistical Manual of Mental Disorders*, or DSM, contained only hints of a disorder resembling Autism. The original DSM-I came out in 1952; its first major revision was in 1968 (DSM-II). Neither volume lists Autism or Asperger's Syndrome; that had to wait for 1980 (DSM-III). The DSM was—and remains—the bible: the book on the shelves of general practitioners, pediatricians, psychologists, and psychiatrists. It was referenced by psychologists and psychiatrists when faced with the signs and symptoms presented by children such as Eileen.

I often think that the fairy child explanation makes as much sense as anything else. Had I known the stories about fairy children at the time, I might have believed that I had a special fairy playmate. I might have felt lucky to have a fairy sister rather than a human one.

SNOW FOR CHRISTMAS

Christmas snow white like frosting on my birthday cake

White like sparkles

Christmas snow sparkles like stars

Christmas stars

Christmas stars in the dark, dark blue

Christmas bulbs all colors, blue as the sky

Some green, green like my Christmas tree.

A Christmas tree tall and big.

Presents, Christmas presents for all the children everywhere

Christmas snow sparkling everywhere

-Eileen

Chapter 2
Learning to Think

Lily and Albert

In 1928, a twenty-three year-old woman named Lyyli Kokko traveled alone from her native Finland, after World War I had decimated the young male population there. She was proud of the fact that she didn't go through Ellis Island because she already had a job  waiting for her. Her name was not readily spelled or pronounced by Americans, so Lyyli became Lily. She might have had a comfortable life in Finland, although her chances of getting married would have been slim. Her connections got her a job on the kitchen staff of a wealthy New York City family. The wealthy family also maintained a summer home on the Connecticut shore.

Lily enjoyed the adventure of her life in the big city in the new world. When her employers went to the shore each summer, they took the servants with them. The vacation house in New London had beaches on the Thames River where it became a broad estuary, on that part of the Atlantic Ocean known as Long Island Sound. The vacation home was a vast Gilded Age mansion that required a large staff. Lily was one of the assistants to the chef.

Two tall Italian men, who grew up helping their father with the landscaping at the nearby Palmer Estate, took care of the grounds at the New London vacation home. They were Albert and his brother Augustus, usually called Al and Gus. They went to the kitchen door for water. Lily met them there. These sweaty young men were thirsty from working in the hot sun. They got water, food, and friendship. Lily gave them the dregs of ice cream that had been hand-churned in a bucket of rock salt for the aristocratic employers.

English was the second language for all of them. Although he was born in the US, Albert Menghi was one of those first generation children who did not learn English until they went to school. Albert grew up in the servant's quarters behind the Palmer Estate in New London. This was an impressive structure, built on wealth accumulated from the textile industry. His father, Alberto was the groundskeeper of the place. Albert, the oldest son, was twenty-two years-old and still living at the Palmer Estate when he and Gus mowed the spacious lawns of the grand vacation home, within walking distance to the estate which was owned by Lily's employer. It wasn't long after that meeting at the kitchen door that Albert Menghi and Lily Kokko married.

Albert had secured a position as gardener at yet another estate. This job included the benefit of a small house behind the mansion. He went to New York and married Lily Kokko at City Hall in Manhattan. He took her back to his little servant home and they had two children: Lily Virginia Menghi, and Albert Oscar Menghi. Virginia and her little brother spent the earliest part of their childhood there. Lily and Albert gave their first names to their children but called them by their middle names. Virginia was nicknamed Ginny. Oscar would later insist on being called Al by everyone except his parents and sister.

When Lily became too sick with tuberculosis (TB) to care for her children, Ginny and her little brother were sent to Catholic school the year they lived with Cesera (my maternal Great-Grandmother) and Lena (my maternal Great-Aunt). The first-grade teacher (a nun) told Ginny that if her mother died from the tuberculosis, she was going to burn in hell for not being Catholic. When Oscar stepped off the sidewalk and onto the grass, not knowing that this was forbidden, a nun picked him up by the hair and placed him back. Ginny was horrified. Albert's father Alberto somehow managed to acquire a large house on Pequot Avenue while still working as a gardener at the Palmer Estate. This large home, with a front porch and walk-up attic, was where we visited Lena and Maurice, and Cesera until she passed away.

I don't know how my great-grandfather managed to purchase and maintain this home working as a servant. The large family with three tall, strong sons may have pooled their resources. The First World War brought manufacturing jobs to the area. Factories and machine shops made all kinds of things for the war in Europe before the US began sending troops. Submarines were being built nearby at Electric Boat. Machine shops hired anyone who could focus and work well with their hands. They may have been given a generous bonus when in 1926, the socialites Theodora and Virginia Palmer, heiresses to the estate, liquidated it and traveled the world to engage in philanthropic activities. Or maybe they were very good at saving money.

1938 was the year that Lily came down with tuberculosis (TB). Maurice was seeking work as a butler, and Lena was taking care of her mother Cesera when they took in six year-old Ginny and four year-old Oscar. Albert moved into a rooming house and worked two jobs to pay the sanatorium fees and to pay his mother and sister for the care of his children. Ginny told me that Cesera and Lena prepared an itemized bill for her father, including things like broken shoelaces and every bite of food Ginny and Oscar ate.

They weren't allowed to talk to their mother in the sanatorium by phone, because Cesera thought the TB germs could go through the wire and infect them, or perhaps she was just cruel. On his day off Albert would take his children for a drive and they would wave to Lily, who would wave back to them from a balcony.

I would learn that Albert was nearly done building a house for his family when the TB hit. He planned to start a plant nursery and sell what he grew on the grounds near the new home. Instead, his mother, father, and sister took over paying the bills on that house, took ownership, and then sold it. He was never able to recover it. Cesera and Lena were not eager to return his son either. They didn't want to keep Ginny, but they spoiled little Oscar. Lily was strong enough to beat TB. She also survived the wacky treatments in vogue before streptomycin was found to be an effective treatment. Sanatorium residents were encouraged to spend time outdoors in their underwear sunbathing, all-year-round. They were subjected to experimental lung surgery as well.

Lily recovered and lived to be nearly ninety-eight years old. She tumbled down a flight of stairs in her late eighties and didn't break any bones. She was made of strong stuff.

The Finns have a word sisu, pronounced as "sissiew," which they say while flexing their muscles. Roughly translated it means strength and resilience. The Finns resisted Russian armies ten times as large as theirs, in sub-zero weather in the dark Arctic winter during the Great War (WWI). Maurice was listed on his draft card as 6'3". Although he was in his late

20s when World War II started, unmarried with no children, he did not serve in the Armed Forces. They may have thought that he was gay; he behaved as if he was gay. Late in life, he had a bedroom made up in the attic of the house for a young man with whom he had a relationship.

I knew Maurice as an eccentric old gentleman who loved opera, painted pictures and was over-dressed for all occasions. He wore ties with clips when he was at home all day. He spent most of his professional life working as a butler or chauffeur, appreciating the finer things left over from his post-Gilded Age employers.

Albert got his family back. He also got a steady job as the head groundskeeper at the US Coast Guard Academy (A federal job with benefits!). His job required him to supervise laborers who mowed the grass and trimmed the hedges. He purchased a little house which had been a historic bowling alley along with the living room with the oddly tilted floor. When I was little, we would visit the strange little house on weekends or holidays. When he had not yet retired, he would often smile and say, "Do you want to go to the greenhouse with me?" The plants needed care every day, so we went. He seemed happy there.

In the greenhouse, he raised the bedding plants that would fill the Academy campus with color all summer. He grew flowering plants and made arrangements for events, dinners held for graduations, and other ceremonies. On these trips we took to the greenhouse, he would open and close windows, snip and water the plants. He introduced his grandchildren to plants and introduced the plants to us kids. I can still remember the way the greenhouse smelled: like earth, humidity, and fresh flowers. He retired and collected a pension that enabled him to spend time cultivating his yard.

He grew prize-winning Dahlias along with all the vegetables he and grandma needed for themselves and all the neighbors. He arranged flowers for my wedding in 1983 and gardened until he died twenty years later, just short of age ninety-three.

My great-uncles Augustus and Maurice also grew vegetables and abundant flowers. Maurice would take this talent in a whole new direction. He created topiaries and fountains in the deep backyard where his parents Alberto and Cesera once lived. Maurice and Lena cared for this house until they were ancient. We visited them on holidays as if they were another set of grandparents.

In the 1990s I returned to that house with my own children. I told them it was the home where their great-great-grandparents had lived. Lena gave my son a hockey stick she had played with in her youth. The attic held many treasures like that hockey stick.

The compulsion to grow food and flowers is a trait that may be as much genetic as learned. I continue to grow food, flowers, herbs, and have a lush edible landscape. When people stop to admire my urban yard and talk to me as they wander by, they often ask if I do all the gardening myself. I sometimes say that gardening is a genetic disorder and I can't help it. Sometimes I tell them that I have billions of worms under the soil doing much of the work.

Now it is 2018. My Brother Tim and I are selling off all the antiques and collectibles that Maurice gathered and stored in his parents' house, and which wound up in my parents' house. My son gave a diamond from Maurice's collection to his fiancée. When she asked about the diamond's history, I told her she might not want to know because Maurice was suspected of nefarious behavior. When Ginny's younger brother Al was still being called by his middle name Oscar, he raised rabbits in a hutch and sold them for meat and fur. He was just a teenager at the time. I recently found out that "Oscar" was also the name of the ship that carried Lyyli Kokko from Finland to the United States.

Sweet Old Dandy

By the time I started school, my sister had been asked to leave. It was 1962. Public schools could refuse to educate students who did not fit into programs designed for typical children. There were some school programs for intellectually disabled children, but they were rare. Families were still being encouraged to put their disabled children into institutions, where they could be ignored and forgotten. Before 1964, when the laws changed and schools were required to provide education for all students, Eileen worked with a private tutor for a few hours each week. Her name was Mrs. Rogers but Eileen called her "Sweet Old Dandy." She was a jolly, retired school teacher making a few extra dollars tutoring part-time. Our parents paid for her services.

She was kind and patient with Eileen. She taught Eileen to read and write at an elementary level. The verse above is a piece of Eileen's spoken poetry, which Sweet Old Dandy assembled into books that Eileen illustrated. One of these poems was even submitted and accepted for publication in the Farmington Valley Herald, the local paper. I was in the car when Ginny picked Eileen up from the tutor. I remember seeing this plump woman at the front door of her house hugging Eileen. She hugged her back and Eileen hugging anyone was remarkable.

We ate dinner out at an Italian restaurant almost every week. Stray cats lived behind that restaurant. We took home a little fluffy orange fleabag of a kitten. He was a sorry little boy with out-turned paws and legs bowed by rickets. He was my cat, and I named him Meteor, because I was seven years old and thought he looked like a glowing ball that might fly through space. He had a pathetic little cry that Eileen imitated. When she heard his pitiful mew, she said "me." The two of them would echo back and forth, *"mew" "me…" "Mew" "me…"* Nobody called the cat Meteor after that. His new name was Memee.

The headhunting business did well. The family looked well and prosperous. We sometimes attended the local Catholic church all dressed up, and Eileen and I sometimes wore matching dresses. All the ladies and girls had to wear hats in church. The men wore hats to church too, but took them off when they stepped inside.

Our living room featured a hi-fi record player and our parents played jazz and Frank Sinatra records. They hosted cocktail parties. Lovely suburban house: check! Three kids: check! Swimming pool: check! All we needed was a dog to have the perfect suburban stereotype. Jack had a pet dog when he was a boy and he wanted a dog now, so he bought a pure-bred boxer puppy and named him Pal. I remember how soft and squirmy he was. Shortly after Pal's arrival he was taken away. He returned with a cropped tail and bandaged ears. I remember crying. I would feel sorry for Pal every time I looked at his ears and tail.

At an early age, I remember thinking that emotions or "feelings" as I referred to them then, were contained in the throat. When I had hurt feelings and was about to cry, I felt a lump or tightening in my throat. So I believed feelings or emotions were located in people's throats. Once while petting the dog, I noticed that the skin and fur at Pal's throat were unusually soft and velvety. I reported that "Pal has fuzzy feelings." Jack thought this was an adorable thing to say and repeated it often. I was annoyed by this because he did not understand what I meant, but I was too young to explain myself.

Memee, the cat, stayed tiny and easily spooked, but he was fluffy and willing to put up with being stroked and cuddled by his little human overlords. Eileen liked to place her arms on either side of him while he lay patiently on her lap. Memee came running home when other cats in the neighborhood bullied him. He was often unable to keep up with grooming his voluminous fur and often sported balls of cat litter on his furry little butt near his furry little testicles.

Pal was very interested in Memee too. Pal would chase little Memee into a corner and hold him down with one paw. Memee froze in terror as Pal sucked on his fluffy tail for a while and then let Memee go. Poor Memee would skitter away, seemingly embarrassed by his slobber-slicked tail.

Ginny had read a book called *How To Give Your Child A Superior Mind*. She used that book and her teacher training to encourage Danny and me to read and explore. We took field trips to swamps and collected bugs, frogs, and toads. Ginny bought field guides and helped us to identify and learn more about the local flora and fauna. She gave us educational games and science kits, and she took us to libraries and museums.

Some of our toys would later be determined to be dangerous. We had the famous creepy crawler "Thing Maker." It was an oven with metal molds. We squirted colored liquid called "plastic goop" into the molds and heated them in the oven. The molds got hot enough to burn you if you failed to use the detachable handle. After cooking these molds to scorching hot, you took them out and waited for them to cool. The goop turned into little rubber bugs and reptiles that would stick to windows and other shiny surfaces. Eileen and I got the 'Fun Flowers' set of molds (sold separately) for the Thing Maker. We made brightly colored rubbery flowers to stick to the large mirror in our shared bedroom.

With Ginny's encouragement, we explored the undeveloped areas around our neighborhood and collected things. She encouraged us to build pens and terrariums for the frogs, toads, and salamanders we hunted and brought home. Jack taught us to swim and he played with us in the swimming pool.

I remember how Jack liked to start his day with a good sneeze before his coffee. Sometimes, he needed the help of bright light. His nose would twitch while his eyes were seeking light. One morning he opened the front door and released a great "At-choo!" into the morning sun in the front yard. Danny and I laughed. Sometime after that, Ginny found an article in the newspaper which reported that light in the eye could make people sneeze because the optic nerve passes the sinuses on the way to the visual cortex. A strong signal like bright light can trigger sneezing in many people—especially when there is already a little tickle, but not quite enough to cause a sneeze. There was an explanation for Jack's sneezing at the light, and a light went on in my mind! This fact piqued my interest in science, and in reading.

The idea that there were explanations for the odd things that people did, and that there were those who spent their careers finding this stuff out, captured my imagination. All through school my favorite subjects would be art, science, and music. As I grew old enough to think about how I wanted to spend my life, it was clear to me that music and art were fun, but knowledge was useful. Science was interesting. I wanted to do something meaningful and valuable. I wanted to find the secrets to my sister's strange transformation. I hoped to find ways to reach her and others like her or at least help them be happy and comfortable.

But when I entered middle school, and slumped into depression and under-achievement, my prospects for a life of science and research dimmed. I withdrew into literature and non-fiction as an escape from homework assignments and thinking about myself. I folded my awkward body and ever-lengthening limbs into the large chair by the hanging lamp in the living room where the TV played talk shows, news, and football games I read book after book.

Ginny would fuss at me for reading too close to my face or in light that was too dim. "Stop reading in the dark, you'll ruin your eyes!" or, "Why is that book so close to your face? You'll ruin your eyes!" I ruined my eyes, just as she warned me I would. After years of textbooks, recreational, and work-related reading, by age forty-seven, my eyes were indeed ruined, like most middle-aged people. I started wearing reading glasses and kept on reading.

Differing Perspectives

When I was three or four years-old, and pictures were being taken, I once posed and said, "Take a picture of me saying a dirty word." That was a story that Ginny often told to illustrate what a bratty child I was from an early age. It was not a "How cute was that?" type of story; it was a "Can you believe this kid?" type of story.

I didn't recall actually saying it, but I could not refute it when she told the story. Ginny's side of each story was the only acceptable side, so I was never able to defend the toddler who allegedly wanted to say naughty things to a camera—even after I learned many years later why I had said it.

It happened like this: Jack did this off-color thing when he had the duty of taking group pictures. To get everyone to smile, he did a twist on the practice of telling people to, "Say cheese." He would instead tell them, "Smile and say shit." This worked really well for getting people to smile, especially at formal occasions in the 1950s when such language was more shocking and unexpected. I must have heard him do this, or overheard a story about it.

He had pretty much stopped doing it by the time his kids were learning to talk. I must have witnessed it or heard about it before I could fully understand it. When I heard this anecdote much later in my life, it provided a different explanation about why little three-year-old me might say, "Take a picture of me saying a dirty word." So maybe that bratty little kid was actually a perceptive little kid. One who assumed that picture-taking is a time to say a dirty word. I at least knew enough not to actually say the dirty word.

Jack grew up poor. His father was probably an alcoholic. His mother was a salty, tough-talking woman. Both his parents smoked cigarettes all the time. His father died of some illness referred to as *consumption* (unspecified and possibly, any number of fatal diseases) when Jack was two years-old. Jack was an ambitious sort who strove to better his life, and rising upward in class meant marrying a classy, educated woman. He and Ginny were the first in their families to complete college. Like many social climbers, they set high standards for language and behavior in their new family. Ginny was the enforcer of these standards with my father's support most of the time.

Jack was impulsive in his humor and temper. He was prone to slipping into inappropriate language and behavior. When he told off-color jokes or made a crude remark, he would get a look from Ginny that Danny named *the hairy eyeball*. When Danny or I were playing too much or being too silly and caught a glimpse of Ginny's look, he'd whisper, "Oh oh look, Mom's giving us the hairy eyeball!"

Once when I was four or five, my father was fashioning the concrete patio that would surround our new pool. He stirred up the concrete mix, water, and sand in a wheelbarrow, and then poured it into wooden frames. I watched while he worked.

I recall this next incident distinctly. He told me, "Go get a bag of cement out of the car will ya?" I went around to the front of the house and tried to move the fifty-pound bag of cement off the tailgate of the station wagon. I could not budge it. I did not realize it weighed more than me at the time, but I tried and tried to do what my daddy wanted me to do. I don't know how long I struggled to move that bag. Jack found me, soaked in sweat, crying with frustration, because I couldn't move the bag of cement—not even an inch. He said he was just kidding, hoisted the bag over his shoulder and continued making the patio. Jack's sense of humor had a cruel edge, even when he was sober.

My parents did their best to cope with a first-born child who was impervious to discipline and two younger children who followed her example when it seemed like fun. One of those problem behaviors was jumping on beds. If Eileen

started, we joined her. She had odd things to sing and shout while we bounced along.

To give us something more acceptable to bounce on, Eileen was given a pogo stick for Christmas, but none of us weighed enough to make it work. When we tried jumping on the pedals, the spring barely flexed at all, and we soon tipped sideways off of it. Jack tried to show us how to use it, but he weighed too much: when he jumped on it, the spring compressed all the way to the bottom and wasn't strong enough to bounce his weight back up. The pogo stick gathered dust until I was big enough to use it. At age ten I would see if I could make it to 1,000 bounces without stopping.

Jack eventually tried another creative solution to the bed bouncing. It worked, but not until the mattress had some broken springs. Our backyard soon acquired a slightly-used trampoline from a recreation center called Jump City. This place went out of business due to accident

liability. People had been willing to pay to jump on trampolines, but when they required hospitalization after getting hurt, they tended to sue for damages, and Jump City bounced out of business.

Jack made the trampoline safer by digging a pit and placing the trampoline at ground level over the hole. This way, if any of us kids bounced off the thing, we didn't fall very far, and we landed on the soft grass surrounding the pit. Jack demonstrated how to do seat drops, flips, and other tricks on the trampoline. He continued to be playfully athletic until well past middle age.

The swimming pool and trampoline made my brother and me more popular than we may otherwise have been, had we relied only on our personalities. Neighborhood kids came to play in our backyard all summer long. After playing in the pool and jumping on the trampoline, a crowd of boys and girls would lie in the sun on the trampoline, courting future cases of skin cancer. We rarely bathed or showered in the summer. Daily swimming in chlorinated water kept us clean enough. The sun and chlorine highlighted our hair. Our tan skin was considered healthy and attractive.

Many of my childhood and adolescent evenings were spent slowly sprinkling chlorine granules around the pool edge each summer. I used a long handled brush to push detritus and chlorine toward the drain in the deep end that led to the filter. Then I skimmed the bugs and other flotsam off the surface. Sometimes I found frogs, toads, moles, or birds floating in the pool. I threw those over the back fence. Because of the steep slope of undeveloped land beyond our yard, the dead critters could decompose beyond where we could see or smell them.

The pool froze in the winter, and sometimes we skated on it. It was way too small but we did it anyway. The swamp at the other side of the housing development made a much better skating rink. There was also a large paved area near the Tariffville Fire Department that was flooded each winter and used as a skating rink. It was like a level parking lot, but it had a curb all the way around it.

In the summertime at the same paved area, the volunteer firefighters hosted a carnival every year to raise money to pay for their equipment. For a few days each summer a bunch of rusty carnival equipment appeared. These fundraisers eventually paid for a wood-burning fireplace near the skating rink/carnival grounds. This way we could warm up by the fire after skating, rather than going home when we got too cold.

The volunteer firefighters took turns hanging out at the old red stone firehouse and drank a lot of beer. They were the kind of guys who would take the fire truck out and use the extension ladder to rescue treed kittens as needed. Once in a while, they also put out fires and cleaned up after bad car accidents.

Living on our block, there was a family of tall blond folks named Shuster. Their father had an Austrian accent, and they owned a Volkswagen. Jack referred to the Shuster's Volkswagen beetle as a "Nazi footlocker." As we made friends in the neighborhood, we reenacted World War II on the playgrounds and in the yards, with toy guns. We insisted that the Shuster boys play the Germans. We killed each other again and again.

Then there was the Italian-American family across the street, with three boys a bit younger than me. They were also close in age: Steven, Christopher, and Robert. We all heard their mother call their names in a New York accent, when she called them home: "Steeeven!" "Christafa!" "Raaabit!" These boys looked up to Danny, who was two years older than the oldest boy, Steven. Ginny gave Danny's outgrown clothes to them. They were proud to wear what they called "Danny shirts." After getting stuck up in a tree, Steven cried so hard when he tore his Danny shirt we all thought he was severely hurt. He wasn't injured, just upset about the shirt. His mother promised to mend it, and he stopped crying.

Before I started school, I gave no thought to how my mother cut my hair. She cut Eileen's hair the same way, and I

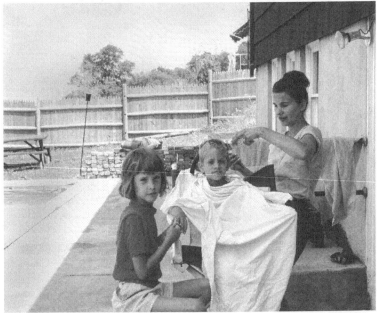

recall enjoying being mistaken for my big sister's twin, feeling flattered. But then when I got to school, I saw some girls had long braids, some did not have bangs, some wore one or two ponytails. I envied the variety of hairstyles my classmates had.

I began to ask if I could grow my hair longer. The answer was no. Ginny told me that I would not be able to take care of long hair properly and refused to let me prove that I could.

I wanted to stop wearing bangs, but Ginny told me that I needed bangs to cover my low forehead. She insisted that my round face required that haircut because of the roundness and disproportion of my short forehead.

It was hard for me to argue with her. My face apparently lacked the perfection of hers, but I just wanted to change my hairstyle. If my face was so wrong why did my hairstyle matter, I wondered? I could look in the mirror and sometimes see that my face was sort of round and my forehead was not as perfect as my mother's but I wasn't sure why this was a problem. Nobody was telling me I was pretty but I didn't care that much because, as a kid, I had better things to do than worry about my appearance. I just envied the other girls who had various hairstyles and had some choice in the matter.

Daydreaming

When I started Kindergarten, and for my first few years of elementary school, I had a habit of pulling my lower lip into my mouth when I was concentrating. In the winter, this often led to chapped and irritated skin around my lip and chin. The skin irritation then made me more likely to tuck my lip into my mouth, especially in the winter. I did this unknowingly as I daydreamed, or thought about things kids think about: Does the air get specks of darkness at night? Is that what darkness is? Can I see the air I breathe? Why does Eileen talk and giggle to herself? Is she talking to someone I can't see?

Ginny would see me with my lower lip in my mouth and sharply say, "Stop chewing on your lip, you're going to look like a Ubangi!" (She pronounced it You Banggee). She showed me pictures of Africans in National Geographic, of women with plates in their lower lips, trying to scare me into believing that I would look like them if I kept chewing my lip.

While I found the interruption of my thoughts and her hard tone of voice irritating, I never believed I was in danger of turning into a half-naked black woman with a big plate inserted into a hole between my lower lip and my chin so that my stretched-out lip held it in place. She showed me the pictures, again and again, each time warning me that I would look just like the big, dark, floppy-breasted women if I didn't stop it. I was not impressed or worried.

I guess it was her version of the parental so-called truism, "Don't cross your eyes or they will stay that way." She didn't do that, or the one about making an ugly face and getting stuck with it. She kept telling me that I looked like, or was going to look like, a Ubangi. I finally looked up Ubangi to see if I could find out when they appeared in the *National Geographic* and found out that they didn't exist. P.T. Barnum's sideshow featured Africans, (purportedly from various tribes and places—although many were former slaves) with lip plates. He chose the geographical name *Ubangi* because it sounded funny to him. I wondered why she didn't just get me some lip balm.

Tariffville and Camelot

Tariffville was part of one of the earliest settlements in New England. The Connecticut River brought settlers to a location that would later be named Hartford. The Massaco river led to an area populated by the Massacco Indians. Settlers began to farm and harvest tar from pine trees in this area in 1630. There were several skirmishes with Indians, who liked to burn the British settlements to the ground. There was a beautiful view from a ridge known as Talcott Mountain, from which the legendary Indian leader King Philip would watch the settlements burn.

By 1676, the Indians had died of European diseases, killed, or moved away. Some colonial neighborhoods and regions bore their tribal names. At a bend in the river, now renamed the Farmington River, there was a small village that developed around a carpet factory. Goods manufactured in the new world were exempt from the taxes, or Tariffs, levied on imported goods to pay for the Revolutionary War, thanks to the Tariff Act. In honor of this, the factory was named the Tariff Carpet Factory.

The Tariff Carpet Factory used the power of the river rapids. The village that sprang up around it was called Tariffville. While it was part of a larger town called Simsbury, it was separated from this town by the river, and later by a railroad track. It was hemmed in by a steep hill on the east side, the river on the north and west side and a floodplain on the south side. Tariffville never grew beyond the less than square mile footprint of the original settlement.

In the mid-twentieth century, the race to suburbia prompted the Hayes family (who had farmed this area since 1640) to sell their land to developers. The resulting housing development had a street named Hayes Road. The descendants of the Hayes family lived in the neighborhood and went to school with my family. Tariffville School was tiny and only went up as far as fifth grade. After that, we took buses across the river and railroad tracks to Simsbury for middle and high school.

Simsbury also had streets and sections named after its original settlers. The fact that there were kids in my class with settler's names made fourth-grade local history classes memorable. There were graves of these early settlers in the local cemetery. I would eventually spend a lot of time at those graves.

The post-war prosperity boom together with their rich histories, made Tariffville and Simsbury seem like legendary, idyllic places to me during my early childhood. Many of the fathers had good paying jobs at nearby companies that quietly made high-tech weapons. They came home to wives who devoted themselves to their homes and broods of children, who in turn had free rein over the verdant lawns, empty lots, and areas too steep or damp to build on. The families attended quaint churches built more than one hundred years ago.

The handsome young President and his beautiful wife gave a sense of glamour to the era and the White House, which for a brief time would be called Camelot. The first family was good looking and young. My family bore a superficial resemblance to them. We too are long-limbed people with thick brown hair. Ginny had beautiful and exotic good looks and brown eyes. President John F. Kennedy had a little girl my age named Caroline. My father was tall and skinny with dark wavy hair and a row of front teeth that looked like piano keys.

He got those teeth in the Navy, after an accident during a submarine diving drill. He was standing watch on deck with binoculars hanging from his neck. The diving drill required him to hurry through a hatch and slide down a ladder quickly. The binoculars caught on a rung and smashed his front teeth upward into his top jaw. When the jaw became infected, he was ordered by a Navy dentist to sit still while his teeth were removed. He was eventually fitted with a dental bridge that looked like piano keys. When he was close to ninety-years-old and Dementia set in, he began obsessing out loud about suing the guy who punched him in the mouth and knocked out all of his front teeth.

There are pictures of Jack as a teenager, with front teeth that did not look like the keys of a piano, but more like the varied teeth that grew in his children's mouths. The teeth in his earlier photographs were mismatched. The later story may have had some truth to it; he may have been bullied by the dentist. Either way, this was a painful and humiliating experience, but the bridge that replaced the teeth he resented losing looked much better than what nature had given him.

I myself had a big gap between my two front teeth, which allowed me to squirt a stream of pool-water six or seven feet. As my molar teeth emerged, that gap closed. My siblings got fangs when their eyeteeth were pushed out of alignment as their molars appeared. I didn't get the vampire fangs. It would have been nice if we had orthodontia to correct our teeth. While my teeth looked to be in alignment, my overbite would become problematic when I was an adult, and by then it was too late to fix it.

The first lady wore top of the line fashions and made the pill-box hat famous. Ginny also dressed well and had a nice ivory-colored suit with an A-line skirt and an imitation leopard hat. The first lady was part French, Irish and Scottish. Ginny also had an uncommon ethnicity, being half Italian and half Finnish. This gave her Scandinavian features with dark coloring. Being relatively tall and voluptuous she was quite striking, especially in the dark red lipstick, shimmery blue eye shadow and dark brown eyeliner she wore during most of her waking hours. I still have trouble picturing her without that makeup.

It was the age of Camelot for the Kennedys and the Hogans. I remember how itchy my good dress was when we went to see the musical Camelot at the Hartford Stage Company. Robert Goulet played Lancelot in the touring company, and my mother had a crush on him. I must have fallen asleep during the second act, because I remember the beginning of the show but not the end.

There was one more similarity. My parents had a convertible. President Kennedy was killed in a convertible. I was sent home from first grade in 1963 on November 22nd because Caroline's daddy had been shot. Caroline Kennedy and I were both six when her father died. The day President Kennedy was shot my mother turned thirty-one years old. I didn't even know it was her birthday. Her age, and even her full name were secrets that she kept from me. I was twenty-three when I learned my mother's name. It was 1980, I had joined the Navy, and I needed to provide this information so that I could receive a top-secret security clearance.

Bells, Smells and Hell: The Catholic Influence

I think my parents did the right thing in the way they offered the option of religion to us. Both had good reasons to doubt, disagree with, and dislike the Catholic faith they had been raised in. They thought it was important to give their children an opportunity to belong to a church and be religious because they believed some people found religion useful or valuable. It also gave us an identity that made us less likely to be outcasts in a small community. They introduced us to our cultural, religious roots, and then did the bare minimum to provide us with enough instruction and ritual to be able to consider ourselves Catholic. They also made it clear that this was not something we were expected to keep doing unless we found it valuable in some way.

We didn't go to Mass every Sunday or holy day of obligation. We weren't Christmas and Easter-only attendees either. We rarely attended church on Christmas, but usually got there on Easter when I was young. We all got dressed up like a good suburban family. Before Vatican II women and girls had to have something on their heads because, as disgusting venal creatures (like Eve), responsible for the downfall of mankind we needed to cover our heads. For Easter, that meant a cap that was made of wire and silk flowers made to clamp onto our heads, chosen to coordinate with the matching outfits my sister and I wore.

For regular Sunday services, we wore lace mantillas. Ginny's was a dramatic black lace triangle draped over her done up hair, the corners swinging prettily down the sides and back. Eileen and I wore smaller white lace mantillas, draped over our matching page-boy haircuts. When I was a gangly teenager with a long mass of bushy brown hair, I tied that white lace mantilla around my head in the back, so it served as a hair band, keeping the hair out of my face. It was fairly ratty by then, but it fit the hippie-chic fashions of the times.

My mother had some deep issues with the church that she rarely spoke about. Parts of her story slipped out, a little at a time over the years. Her parents were a scandalous mixed-religion couple. Albert, her Italian Catholic father, had eloped with Lily Kokko, a Finnish Lutheran. I was told that in order to marry in a Catholic church, she had to promise to raise her children Catholic.

After my grandparents died in 2003, my mother found documents in their home which indicated that they didn't have a Catholic Church wedding. They had secretly eloped on a trip to New York. This was never spoken about at family reunions, and even my mother had to wait until after her parents died to put these pieces together.

For my grandmother, raising her children Catholic was probably done in deference to the large Italian family and community she had married into. As the only Finnish Lutheran in the Little Italy community, she went along with the majority. I don't believe religion was relevant at all to my grandparents. They didn't have any religious icons or pictures around their house. They only went to church for funerals and weddings when I knew them.

My formal religious education began in second-grade Catechism class. My older brother and sister were in the same class. The church used the local elementary school for these classes, and the teachers were volunteers culled from the more devout or willing parents of the congregation. We kids had skipped first-grade indoctrination; probably, because of the trauma Ginny experienced learning about Hell and her own Lutheran mother's eternal damnation. All three of us went into the same classroom because Eileen and Danny had not yet attended Catechism. Ginny came and stayed with us in class because Eileen was unpredictable and might unexpectedly wander off. The deacons in charge of the Catechism program were also the administrators of the local public schools, who had banished Eileen from second grade and suggested she be placed in a mental institution.

Ginny may also have wanted to monitor the horrific nature of some Catholic teachings so that she could reassure her children that most of it wasn't true. Both of our parents made it clear that we went to the Catholic Church because it was where our family celebrated weddings and funerals. They

56

thought that there was some value in belonging to a church, but they assured us there was more than one way to be a good person. They also made it clear that they didn't agree with the Pope about what was right or wrong. They never hid their belief that good non-Catholics deserved heaven as much as Catholics did.

We had no idea how seriously other Catholics took their religion, going to church every single week and on holy days of obligation. We never got ashes smeared on our foreheads on Ash Wednesday like most of the other Catholics in our neighborhood. There was another church in Tariffville. It was Episcopal and made of dark red stone. It was on the same block as our pretty white church. The few Jewish neighbors had to travel to West Hartford, where some impressive synagogues stood.

Second grade was when they began to prepare us for First Holy Communion. Danny and I would participate by learning how to confess our sins in the closet at the back of the church on Saturday, then skip breakfast and have a little wafer in church on Sunday. This would allow us to avoid eternal damnation if we happened to die suddenly. Eileen did not continue in Catechism class after that year. The deacons, who had also kicked Eileen out of school for being exactly the way God made her, apparently considered her not worthy of salvation due to her tendency to disobey orders and wander away when she felt like it. Ginny was too busy to sit in class with Eileen if her daughter wasn't welcome to participate in any rituals or sacraments.

This struck me as unfair. I had only just learned that Santa Claus was a lie. Ginny and Jack made a big deal about Santa. It seems they started warning us in August that if we didn't behave we would get lumps of coal in our stockings rather than presents for Christmas. Jack went so far as to climb up on the roof and pretend to be Santa shouting, "Hohoho" down the chimney and conversing with us, while we talked into the fireplace down below and told him what we wanted. Always, the Christmas presents were promised on

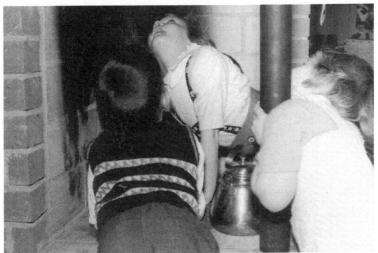

the condition that we were good. When I learned that Santa was a myth, I thought the whole ruse was a bribe to trick children into being good. It never occurred to me that we got presents no matter how we behaved. We never saw a lump of coal until we got a geology kit for Christmas.

I began to suspect that the heaven and hell stories were another trick; this one, to fool adults into behaving well. There was one tangible indication that the adults truly believed in an all-powerful God. It was that there were so many impressive structures built for Him. I had never seen anything impressive to prop up Santa. The costumed Santas and department store displays were obviously cheap and temporary. The churches though, were beautiful, large, and imposing. The stained glass windows were breathtaking works of art that glowed and transformed as the sunlight shifted outside. This apparently cost some real money and effort on the part of serious adults.

I wondered if they, the adults, were tricked into believing in heaven and hell. I was atheistic decades before I knew there was a word for it. I don't think I was ever a true believer. How could an all-knowing and loving God create problems in a child like Eileen? Problems that made her unable to follow the religious regimen, and then punish her for being the way He made her? Would Eileen burn in hell forever and ever because she couldn't behave well enough to do the communion thing? I knew there were others, people with broken brains and disabilities, who couldn't follow all the Catholic rules even if they wanted to. I also wondered about all the kids in school who followed other religions; the Episcopalians and the Jews.

The idea of living after death was another thing that was hard to fathom. What would you do all day? Where were these places, and wouldn't we have found them by now if they existed? We seem to have explored the planet thoroughly, and telescopes had provided a view of the solar system. Wouldn't a place where God, angels, and billions of souls lived have been obvious?

I did seem to achieve some success from prayer once. In Catechism class there was a drawing one year near Christmas time, a chance to win a big advent candle. The advent candles ritual was not practiced in our home, and the teaching seemed special, because there was some hocus-pocus deal with lighting special candles on certain days until Christmas. Since neither of my parents smoked, the fire element was especially alluring to me.

The Catechism teacher had us all write our names on slips of paper which were then tossed into a bowl, and one name was drawn to win the huge candle. I clasped my hands under my desk, closed my eyes and prayed, "Pleasepleaseplease let it be my name." I went home with a Pillar candle with a symbol on it that looked like a P mixed with an X. It must have weighed five pounds, but I was proud to carry it the three-quarter mile trek home. It was supposed to be placed at the center of the Advent wreath with four smaller candles, to be lit in the weeks leading up to Christmas. This may have been explained in class, in a way that seemed magical. We didn't have an advent wreath at home like good Catholics were supposed to have, so that big candle was never used as it was intended.

Something about fire and rituals ignited my childish imagination. At home, we only had candles ritually lit on birthday cakes. There was a song and a chance to use the power and magic of the birthday ritual to get a wish granted. Catholic rituals with candles were even more exciting because they were done by an exotically attired Priest and altar boys that I only saw in church on Sunday, and the nuns that I only saw in the movie "The Sound of Music."

There were some captivating things about Church. When I was little, the Masses were said in Latin, and although it made no sense to me at all, together with the grandly appointed church filled with candles and stained glass-filtered light, the Latin words seemed like magical incantations. The ringing bells and the burning incense created an atmosphere of mystery. There was something about the way the organist pulled out so many stops that our relatively small rib cages would vibrate with the organ pipes when we opened our mouths and sang that it made me feel filled with something indescribably powerful. I read more about religion, listened to people talk about it, and discussed beliefs and religious practices often as I grew up.

We studied local history in school and learned about the harsh ways of the Puritans, and how they banished the gentle peace-loving Quakers to Pennsylvania where they established Philadelphia, the City of Brotherly Love. I would be influenced by a historical novel, "The Witch of Blackbird Pond" by Elisabeth George Speare. The main character, an intrepid sixteen-year-old girl, travels to a small town on the Connecticut River to unite with her Puritan aunt and uncle after fleeing an arranged marriage to an older man. Because she has some unique ideas and skills, like the ability to swim and read, she has trouble being accepted by her Puritan kin. A jealous and ignorant woman accuses her of witchcraft, and she is nearly killed. Her friends and family, however, have found her to be a kind and helpful woman, and she escapes the torture, drowning, or hanging prescribed by the religious authorities.

I would find myself drawn to stories of those who were set apart and misunderstood. The suppressed people, the unfairly persecuted had voices that spoke louder to me than the authorities of religion. I identified with the rebels, the outcasts, and the underdogs. This mindset would bring me in frequent conflict with my parents, who had become increasingly hardened as patriotic Republican conservatives. But by allowing me to pick and choose my religious beliefs, and by their own refusal to follow established paths to prosperity, they had planted in me the seeds of independence, outside of the box thinking, and creativity.

In order to learn why people seemed to take religion so seriously and why they had impressive facilities that were dedicated to it; I continued praying. I prayed that Eileen would get better and be like other girls. I even offered to give up something in exchange, like my ability to walk or hear. I wanted a sister with a sound mind. I don't know if I wanted this so I could have Eileen as a friend, or if I wanted to gain that sort of magical power promised by those who believed in prayer. The fervent requests and bargains I tried to make with God never seemed to work on Eileen.

Maternal Ancestors

Jack and Ginny both grew up in New London. They attended the same high school but didn't meet until they were both nearly done with college. Jack was almost five years older, but Ginny went straight to college, and Jack detoured through the Navy. Most of my extended family stayed in Southeastern Connecticut while we were living more than an hour away in the northern part of the state. On holidays and summer vacations we visited relatives and the beaches in the New London area. We saw our relatives a few times each year.

When I was little, my great-grandmother was still alive, and we were taken to see her. Her name was Cesera (Chez-a-ray). I was told to call her Nonie. I thought that was her name. Nonie is Italian for grandma. Cesera didn't speak English, and according to census data, she never learned to read or write. Cesera was shrunken; wheelchair bound, and usually had her rheumatoid arthritis misshapen hands on her lap. As a small child, when I was presented to her, my mother's aunt, Lena would translate basic questions and answers, like what grade in school I was in, and other such things that old people ask little kids. Ginny believed that Cesera was exaggerating her pain to keep Lena, her only surviving daughter, and her youngest son Maurice, around to wait on and care for her.

Ginny could be dismissive of other people's ailments. She was very stoical, and didn't cry or take time off for illness. She had little empathy for her grandmother. She nursed some resentment from the time she lived with Cesera while her own mother suffered from tuberculosis.

My great-grandfather Alberto left the seaside town of Fano, Italy at thirteen on a small ship that carried other Italians to Ellis Island. He was identified on the passenger list as a laborer. He may have been taken in by another Italian family. This story was explained late in my grandfather Albert's life, as he began to share the truth about things kept quiet for many years. Maybe Alberto had left home because he was abused or neglected by his family; that was one story.

My great uncle Maurice, who was the nuttiest and most flamboyant member of the family, had a flair for the dramatic, and his stories were regarded with suspicion. He had his own version of why Alberto left Italy alone at age thirteen. Maurice believed that his father was the bastard son of someone in power. If Alberto were to come of age in Italy, his existence would cause power struggles. So the boy who would have been part of some grand political intrigue was carried off to the United States to hide his existence, maintaining the power dynamic. He became one of a family of gardeners and servants instead. This rumor may only have survived because it was amusing and illustrated the generalized weirdness that was great-uncle, Maurice.

Family lore and research show my Italian ancestors as poor and unfortunate. Like many immigrants, they scrambled and scraped to improve their lot in life. Ginny's paternal grandparents were born in Italy and immigrated to New London where they spent the rest of their lives. Their neighborhood was an Italian enclave. They spoke Italian at home, and the children learned to speak English when they went to school. They never moved more than a few blocks away. They recreated the old world community they came from in a section of New London known as Fort Trumbull.

Alberto and Cesera had five children: Albert, Augustus (Gus), Mary, Lena, and Maurice. I would only know four of them, and nobody ever talked about one of the girls. Alberto died in 1945 at age sixty, before I could meet him. Ginny remembered that he was still tall, strong and working when he got appendicitis. He made it through surgery, but died of an infection he caught in the hospital.

Autism II

Autism, as a diagnosis, was a new theory. It was pioneered by the father of child psychiatry, Leo Kanner. Kanner, from Berlin, proposed the term infantile Autism to describe some young children who appeared withdrawn, non-verbal and unable to connect with others. Kanner came to the United States in 1924 and published his work on Infantile Autism in a 1944 paper (Leo Kanner, "Infantile Autism," *The Journal of Pediatrics* 25 [September, 1944], p. 211-217) written while he worked at Johns Hopkins University in Baltimore, Maryland.

Another early researcher was Hans Asperger of Vienna, Austria, who in 1943 wrote the first general definition of Autism. Asperger continued through the 1960s studying unusual children he labeled as Autistic (Frith, Uta. *Autism and Asperger Syndrome*. New York: Cambridge University Press, 1992.).

But Kanner and Asperger's knowledge and theories were not widely known. Only their private patients received the Autism diagnosis. The proper diagnosis of these odd children was thus limited to those families who had the time, energy and means to travel to Baltimore or Vienna. This left a void in knowledge for both the public and the psychiatric communities. Because of the challenge of seeking out one of these experts, Autism was initially assumed to be a rare disorder that only occurred in very accomplished families with exceptional intelligence!

VALENTINES

Valentines like lace

Lace on your dress

Valentines for everybody you love

Work and work to make them pretty

You send them in the mail

The mailman feels happy when he brings them

Today I made valentines for Mother and Father

Big red hearts!

Red like sunshine!

-Eileen

Keeping up with the Hogans

While Ginny was the one in charge of the home, the kids, the shopping, the cooking, the housework, the bookkeeping, the typing, filing and telephones, Jack would occasionally help out – by playing with us kids. He wrestled with Danny on the living room floor. He gave Danny boxing lessons. Jack encouraged Danny's interest in mechanical things and got used or broken go-carts and minibikes for him to tinker with and ride around the empty lots nearby. Jack found ways to make his playthings benefit the family. He loved swimming and diving, so we had a big deep pool. He could swim and play in his pool, and his kids also got to swim and play.

He invented games to play in the pool. One of these games was called "depth charge." It involved a beer can full of pebbles that we carefully dropped off the diving board while one of us swam underwater across the pool pretending to be a submarine. If you dropped the can at the right time, it would hit the swimmer, who then got to be the submarine.

Jack taught us to hyperventilate before swimming underwater and compete to see who could swim the furthest without coming up for air. I was the best at this. I eventually swam four lengths of the pool without coming up for air, beating Jack's record. Sometimes Jack would roughhouse in the pool with us and hold us underwater while we struggled to escape. Once when I grabbed a clump of hair on his leg, and twisted it, the game ended.

Occasionally, his experience as an exhibition diver came out. He was replacing the shingles on the roof one summer.

After working in the hot sun, he stripped down to his shorts and decided he wanted to dive into the pool. The roof was more than two stories above the pool, and there were about 9 feet of concrete separating the edge of the house from the pool. There was only a small area in the pool deep enough for such a high dive, and even that area had a diving board that jutted out over part of it. He could have clasped his knees to his chest in a cannonball, or done a swan dive, but decided to do a double front flip off the roof and into the pool. Ginny saw him flipping past the second story window, and yelled out, "I haven't paid the insurance BILL!"

Being self-employed meant that Jack could take a few weeks off and replace the roof shingles rather than hiring contractors. This lifestyle allowed us to have the biggest house and best swimming pool in the neighborhood, but unlike middle-class families where the parents had professional jobs and steady pay, our bills might pile up unpaid.

The rugged individualism promoted by my parents gave us some advantages as well as disadvantages. We had a swimming pool but lacked regular medical and dental care. Jack did all the car maintenance and repairs he could figure out how to do but we never had our hair cut or styled professionally. Jack built additions that nearly doubled the size of the house as the family grew, but we never had orthodontic care for our over-bites and uneven teeth. College savings accounts were out of the question.

Jack liked boating. I can't call it yachting because he would buy a used boat that needed work. The first boat we had was twenty-eight feet long and technically big enough for all six of us to sleep on. After we scraped the barnacles off the hull and painted the bottom with anti-fouling paint that discouraged the infiltration and attachment of sea creatures and organisms hungry for that wooden hull, it was ready to launch. We could begin taking trips along coastal Connecticut and Rhode Island.

We spent the first few weekends of the spring and summer fixing and painting the boat and then the rest of the summer and early fall weekends enjoying it. We often slept on the boat in the very compact cabin. Eileen and I shared the V-bunks in the bow. These narrow beds were about two feet wide where our heads rested; the bunks joined together (like the letter V) at the front of the boat where our feet rested. We slept in sleeping bags. Danny and Timmy slept on one side of the cabin in bunk beds transformed from the sofa: the back of the sofa flipped up and was suspended by straps to the overhead to form the top bunk.

The dinette where we ate our meals on board converted into a bed for our parents. The table was dropped down between the seats and the seat backs placed on top of the table. Jack had to accept the fact that he snored after all of us verified what Ginny had been telling him for years.

Breathing Trouble

The headhunting business was doing well in 1965. Jack purchased a brand new 1966 Thunderbird. He was thrilled with it. The back seat was not comfortable for three kids however and one of us would have to sit on the hump in the middle while the other two jockeyed for the window seats. It was not as practical as the old station wagon which was Ginny's car.

Two families in our neighborhood considered themselves above the rest. I'll call them Deacon Walters and Gabriel

Deacon. They both had girls that went to school with us. They were administrators in the local schools and Deacons in our Church. Gabriel Deacon sang tenor solos with the choir. To this day, hearing a strong tenor soloist reminds me of him, and it is not a fond memory. Deacon Walters is the one who tried to convince my parents to institutionalize Eileen (in a mental hospital for adults) when she was just a skinny little seven year-old girl.

Elaine Walters was a year ahead of me in school and had been in class with Danny and Eileen before they kicked Eileen out of school. She was a nasty snob of a child then. Elaine had probably been influenced by her father to look down on us. She followed me home from school telling me, "your sister's retarded, your brother's retarded, your whole family's retarded. You even have a retarded dog."

One day when I was eight years old, I was hanging out in my room with my brother, and we were goofing around, as kids do. This day, we were ranting about Elaine Walters. I was performing an impression of this hateful child by doing a silly walk across the room, saying, "do wee, do wee, do wee." I walked knock-kneed while sticking out my butt. I kept up the performance, walking out of the room, then turned back into the room and shut the door. A few moments before that, my mother had summoned me to the kitchen, which was down the hall at the far end of the house.

I was busy doing an eight-year-old's version of performance art, and probably "in the zone" as they say in the creative arts, so I heard nothing. About a minute later, Ginny stormed into the room, in full hairy eyeball mode, and demanded to know:

"Why did you decide to ignore me?"

"I didn't hear you."

"YES, YOU DID!"

"No, I didn't!" It was the only thing I could think of to say.

"You did hear me, and instead of coming, you slammed the door!"

"No, I didn't!"

I'm not sure how many times this went back and forth, before she lost her temper, grabbed my shirt, and slammed the heel of her hand into my face causing my nose to bleed so much that it made me gag. Ginny switched gears got a hold of some cloth and instructed me to lie on my back and pinch my nose. Danny said something, something that supported my side of the story. "Okay. Maybe you didn't," she replied.

After my mother admitted that it was possible I was telling the truth about not being able to hear her, (rather than hearing her and choosing to ignore her) she said she was sorry. Then she followed up with a sharp admonition that I should not have been fooling around in such a way as to be unable to hear her if she had happened to call me.

In retrospect, I think my mother's temper may have been extra short at that particular time. She was dealing with a development that was about to make her life nearly impossible to manage: she was pregnant again.

She was already stretched thin running the house and business while my father traveled. She had finally gotten Eileen into a stable school environment and therefore could spend the time that us three kids were in school to keeping up with business, as well as everything else. She may have been wondering how she was ever going to be able to hold everything together when the baby she was carrying arrived. She had summoned me to come and set the table for dinner.

She was probably freaking out about what she would do if I couldn't be relied upon to help as needed.

My First Funeral

I was nine years old when we went to my great-grandmother's funeral. Timmy was still in the hospital, and Ginny was not yet burdened with round-the-clock care of a sickly baby. It was my first funeral, and I had expected sad faces, and a somber atmosphere that some TV show suggested was appropriate. I was confused when Albert and his siblings were smiling and laughing together like it was a party. I asked my grandfather why they were happy. He told me that his mother had been in pain and now her suffering was over, and that they were glad. Maybe there were other reasons to be happy. Lena and Maurice, the youngest surviving siblings, were now free from the constant care their mother required. Neither of them had married, and now as senior citizens, they could finally share the beautiful home and gardens without supervision and eldercare responsibilities. Some other family secrets and resentments probably went to the grave with Cesera. She married Alberto at age twenty-one on the same day that she arrived from Italy. She may have been sent from the old country to a marriage arranged by family. She certainly suffered from arthritis and old age and there was a child of hers that I never met because she had died at age four after her clothes caught fire at a spring bonfire. She was severely burned, hospitalized, and dead the next day. I wouldn't learn about little Mary Menghi until after I grew up. She was rarely spoken about by those who remembered her.

Depression and sorrow may have been as crippling to Cesera as arthritis. I learned much later that Cesera was afflicted with obsessive hand washing, like Lady Macbeth. The hand washing quirk might be a genetic link to the way my sister and I pull out our hair when under stress. It is the kind of activity seen in unhappy zoo animals, the pacing and excessive grooming that animals in small cages do. Cesera did not read, write, drive or speak English. She was trapped in her home by cultural customs and sorrow as much as by arthritis. Her hand washing may have been related to being trapped, isolated, and in pain.

My sister Eileen would also develop a repertoire of obsessive-compulsive behaviors as she grew up. She stayed at home until she was sixty-two, trapped by mental illness and a controlling mother.

Timmy Comes Home

Ginny would not be able to rest for the next few years. Timmy was born with a collapsed trachea. Ginny was ahead of her time in refusing anesthesia for childbirth. She recalled hearing them say, "It's a boy," and then they clapped a face mask over her nose and mouth to knock her out. When she came to, they explained that they had performed an emergency tracheotomy so that he would be able to breathe until his trachea became firm. This would take most of his first year. He stayed in the intensive care unit until all of my parent's money was used up. This took a little over a month.

Jack told me about looking through a window into the intensive care room where his youngest child was struggling to breathe. He was wondering what would cost more, keeping him in the hospital or the cost of funeral expenses if Timmy died. While he was considering how he would pay for the life or death of his baby, there was a sudden flurry of activity around the bassinet. After things settled down a doctor came out to tell Jack that Timmy had stopped breathing, but they had gotten him breathing and stabilized again. Jack wondered if his thoughts had caused the crisis. This idea sent him running to the restroom to vomit.

Timmy should have stayed in the hospital longer, but the cost of intensive care had used up all the insurance, all the savings, and there was nothing left. Rather than go deeper into debt, Ginny did the intensive care at home. When we brought him home, Timmy was still the size of a newborn, soft and squishy like most babies, but wearing some silver hardware at the base of his neck. The bracket that held the cannula (tube) in place was sterling silver and strapped on with white cotton gauze straps. The straps were tied gently around his squishy baby neck, tight enough to hold the thing up against the stoma in his throat, but not so snug as to depress the arteries in his neck and cut off brain circulation.

Jack said he was dressed formally in a silver bow tie. Noses are self-cleaning. A sneeze will blow out any snot, dust, or whatever else gets in it. Throats can be cleared with a cough. Most babies sneeze and cough regularly and cutely. But when a baby breathes through a tracheal tube, the airway needs to be cleared manually, or breathing stops. If the tube gets clogged, no air gets through. If milk goes down the wrong way, choking doesn't work; and if liquid gets into the lungs, pneumonia ensues.

The suction machine that came home from the hospital with Timmy looked like a prop in a horror movie. It had glass jars, rubber tubes, and a noisy electric pump. The machine sucked mucus out of the curved cannula while it was in Timmy's neck. Ginny sterilized these tubes on the kitchen stove in a saucepan of boiling water. When she changed the tubes every few days, she would have the new sterile tube ready. She'd unclip and gently remove the gloppy phlegm-covered tube out of the bracket at the base of Timmy's neck. She then had to carefully (and quickly) slide the sterilized cannula into this squirming infant's neck so he could breathe again.

As far as I was concerned, Timmy was the best thing my parents ever brought home for me to play with, and we all loved him. He was a quiet baby because he had no air in his vocal chords. Instead of crying loudly, he would turn red and squirm a bit. Ginny continued to take care of the cooking, cleaning and secretarial and administrative duties of the family business along with the infant care and extra medical care Timmy needed.

Jack tried hiring a cleaning lady to come and clean once each week, but Ginny was uncomfortable with someone else seeing our dirt and disorder. She felt compelled to clean up before the cleaning lady came. The cleaning lady once asked me to take out the trash because she was afraid of that dog chained out near the trash cans. Pal was spending more time tied up outside because of the sick baby, and all the other problems. The cleaning lady was let go after a few weeks, and soon Pal was given to a kindly retired man who had time to take care of him.

Timmy was prone to respiratory infections because he was unable to filter out germs the way babies who breathed through noses could. He went to the doctor for frequent illnesses and pneumonia. Sometimes the doctor came to our house. I was too young to take care of him, and taking him out in cold weather was dangerous. In the winter he couldn't just be trundled into the car when Ginny needed to shop or take another kid somewhere.

Jack spent less time traveling and less time working, to be available for emergencies and to take care of some of my mother's many responsibilities while she took care of Timmy. Ginny got very little sleep. She needed to be vigilant all night in case he stopped breathing due to a clogged tube, not to mention the more typical baby needs like changing or feeding. He made no sound when he cried, so Ginny had to rely on hearing the rustling of his squirms—or perhaps extrasensory perception.

Jack would often take us three older kids out for "mystery rides," to give Ginny a break so she could take care of the house and the baby without having three kids aged nine, ten, and eleven clattering around. Sometimes we went to playgrounds. Sometimes we waited in the car while he took care of some business or household issue. We made trips with him to hardware stores and auto parts shops. He was doing most of the repairs himself.

Business was down, savings were gone, and the mortgage still needed to be paid. My parents made an arrangement with the bank to avoid losing the house. They paid only the interest on the mortgage, and in return, the bank did not repossess it. Ginny called the March of Dimes, who advertised for money often on TV in order to help children with birth defects. They agreed that Timmy had a birth defect and would help with finances, but only after the house and cars were gone.

Once I was kept after school for chewing a stick of gum a friend had given me. Ginny had to bundle Timmy into the aging station wagon with faulty heat, in the winter, to pick me up and meet with the vice-principal. She was seething with anger. I had no idea how deadly that car trip must have been for Timmy. I felt the heat of Ginny's rage but only found out years later that the one she was fuming at was the vice-principal. In disciplinary matters, my parents—like most of that era—held a united front with other adults in authority against child misbehavior. She had to pretend she was upset with me rather than the vice-principal who insisted that she come to school and endanger her baby's life, because of a piece of chewing gum. She kept most of that anger at the vice-principal inside, like steam in a pressure cooker. She shared the truth about her anger at the vice-principal with me over fifty years later.

When times were most difficult, Ginny became rigid and tense. Before this time she had three hairstyles. There was the bun, on top but near the back of her head. And there was the French twist, a smooth folded thing on the back of her head that was narrow at the bottom and broad at the top. This elegant 'do gave her the look of an Egyptian Queen with a crown. Then, there was a third style for special occasions. She would set it on rollers and wear it down in big curls held firmly in place with a few bobby pins and a lot of Aqua Net hairspray. The bun and the French twist were also covered with hairspray until nearly solid and held with even more bobby pins. No matter the style, her hair never moved once it was done.

After Timmy was born, the bun became a permanent fixture. She took her hair down to wash it once each week. When she did, it was strange to see how long and straight it was. But just as long straight hair was becoming stylish in the 1960s, she went with a bun all the time. Now, each morning, she swept any stray hairs up, stuck in a few more bobby pins, and sprayed it with more Aqua Net. She covered her face with liquid foundation to hide the minor flaws that only mattered to her, and powdered over the foundation. She applied her dark red lipstick, a line of soft eyeliner and shimmery blue eye shadow. Her eyebrows were always perfectly shaped, and she rarely emerged from her bedroom without her hair and face made up as if she was going off to work at a fashion magazine.

In the same way, her hair and face were sculpted and painted to perfection; her routine became more rigid as well. It was as if her beauty and grooming routine was an attempt to gird her composure with armor for the battle that each day became. She smiled less often and became more short-tempered with Danny and me.

Jack used jokes to deal with difficult times. He often said, "There are too many kids around here. If I ever find out what causes them, I'm going to stop it, whatever it is." He also said, "I should have named you kids Eeny, Meeny, Miney, and Sam. Ya know why? Because we didn't want no Moe."

The Halls lived two doors down the street from us. Dick and Shirley Hall had two girls, Brenda and Lisa, who were one and two years younger than me respectively. We often played together. Dick and Shirley were the kind of people Jack and Ginny liked to be friends with; they enjoyed drinking and listening to jazz. Jack and Ginny wanted to go to the Halls' house for a New Years Eve Party. The neighborhood parents put on their best clothes to ring in the New Year at the Hall's house with cocktails, hors-d'oeuvres, and Frank Sinatra records. Ginny hadn't been out since bringing Timmy home from the hospital. It was snowing heavily, so it was likely that the party-goers would only be those within walking distance.

That night Danny and I were allowed to stay up watching TV until they came home, while Timmy slept on the couch where we could see him. I was almost ten. After Timmy was asleep, Ginny put on her fur coat and sparkling jewelry. I was given strict instructions to call the Hall's if anything went wrong with Timmy.

After about an hour of watching the TV and listening to Timmy breathing, I noticed that he was looking pinker than usual. I felt his forehead, and he seemed warmer than usual. I consulted with Danny, who agreed he was pinker and warmer than usual, so I called the Halls' house, asked to talk to my mother, and reported my concerns about Timmy. A few minutes later both our parents walked in the door, lightly dusted with snow. Mom checked Timmy. She told me, "There was nothing wrong. He's always a little bit pink and warm when he sleeps." Acting irritated that I had called; they went back to the party.

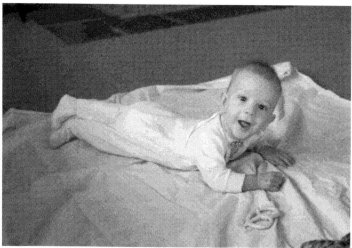

I later learned that Shirley Hall had once offered to babysit Timmy so that Ginny could go out for an evening. Ginny showed her the tracheotomy tubes and explained everything she would have to do if Timmy had trouble breathing. Shirley regretfully admitted that she didn't think she could do what might be needed and retracted her offer.

Once in a while, Eileen would say something interesting or amusing. At the dinner table, Danny was having trouble thinking of a word and said "umm, umm" a few too many times. Eileen piped up helpfully with the word she thought he was searching for, "Umbrella?" It was not the word he was looking for, but the situation was so funny that after that we all began to suggest "Umbrella" anytime someone said "Um." Eileen rarely spoke. She kept to herself and spent time making art. She lurked around like a ghost when the rest of us ate meals or spent time by the pool in the summer.

"I'll Give You Something to Cry About!"

Eileen made it through kindergarten and first grade at Tariffville School. For several years she was either tutored or went to schools that had classes for kids who were not able to fit into in regular classes until she wound up in a laboratory school. In 1966, when Eileen was eleven, and her peers were in fifth grade, she ended up in a class for emotionally disturbed kids, which was part of a laboratory school called the Gengras Center. It served as a training program for special education teachers at St. Joseph's College in West Hartford. School districts that could not educate special needs students could send their more challenging students there. The sending school districts paid tuition and future teachers could train there under the close supervision of an experienced teacher. Eileen had the same teacher every year, and he became a friend of the family. He was welcome to our home, and he brought his boyfriend over to go swimming on a few occasions. I talked much more than my older sister, who had retreated into her own world.

I talked more than Danny. He was introverted. I rattled on about things I had read from magazines and newspapers that came into the house, as well as library books. My talking often annoyed our parents. I never sensed a pattern to what sort of subjects would bring about a sigh or eye roll. Sometimes, Ginny would just say, "Sharon, would you PLEASE stop talking." Other times, after I shared some item from my reading, she would say "Where did you get that from?"

"I read it somewhere."

"Where? Where did you read that?"

"A magazine, I think."

"Yeah, you read it somewhere," she would say, dripping with sarcasm.

If I became emotional in any way when defending my point of view, Jack discouraged any crying with the typical "stop crying or I'll give you something to cry about" threat. He had another way to discourage crying or whining that he seems to have developed himself. He would imitate any crying sounds we made, in a sneering and mocking way. Any attempt to explain why we were upset led to more mocking and fake crying. Laughing at me and mocking me did make me shut up, but it left me seething with anger. If I had an angry outburst, I got hit or severely reprimanded.

Eileen didn't get the same treatment. She didn't cry or change her ways, so there was no point in correcting anything she did. Danny and I learned not to cry very often. I had more trouble learning to shut up than the other kids, so I was most often the target of reprimands, lectures, and ridicule. I tried to keep my feeling to myself when being harangued for being upset. Once when I was eleven years old, after a harsh session of the usual, "Stop crying or I'll give you something to cry about," I went to my room and wrote a letter to my future self. I wanted to remind myself that if I ever had children not to treat them that way because it hurt so much. I wrote in pen on white lined paper in a spiral notebook. The exact words are long lost.

I recall writing that children should be allowed to talk about their motives and feelings, and parents should try to understand them. I went on, covering both sides of a single sheet with my loopy mixture of cursive and print handwriting. I tore the sheet out of my notebook, folded it until it was the size of hotel soap bar and stuffed into a dresser drawer underneath my hairbrush, troll doll, and other odds and ends.

Science Kits and Hula Hoops

I was relatively happy and competent through most of elementary school. At recess, we played with hula hoops and jump ropes. I was good at these things and enjoyed the friendship of other girls. At home, we had books, science kits, arts and craft supplies. We also had a little brother to play with. Danny liked science and once wanted to test what he had learned about how baby bones were flexible, and the skull had fissures took some time to close. He would see how much flex was in Timmy's arm or head until Timmy cried or I told him to stop.

If other kids joined us in the yard, we would play imagination games. One game was based on a TV show about people stranded on a deserted tropical island. "Gilligan's Island" was a situation comedy about a mixed group of people who lived in grass huts and survived on coconuts and fish. I had trouble understanding why they wanted to leave. The weather was always pleasant, and none of them had to work very hard. It seemed like paradise. My friends and I pretended we were stranded on a similar desert island. We made up adventures. We climbed on top of the shed that held the pool supplies and jumped off of it pretending it was a cliff. We pretended the trampoline was quicksand, and we had to bounce our way out of it.

Another game I talked everyone into playing was based on a science fiction movie called *The Last Woman on Earth*. The film depicted three people who survived a temporary lack of oxygen; a married couple, and a single man. These three people survived because they were scuba diving when aliens stole all the oxygen causing the rest of humanity to die.

We imagined having the world to ourselves, free to drive any car, play at any amusement park, and eat any food we could find. In the movie, the two last men killed each other fighting over the woman, and at the end she had the whole planet to herself. It was quite a fantasy for a suburban girl.

These games of adventure and escape seem to have developed as my parents began to disapprove of how other children's parents behaved. I was often invited to my friend's houses, and Ginny would say "no, have your friends play over here." This was usually not a big deal as we had one of the prime play areas in the neighborhood. But sometimes my friends tired of our place and wanted me to hang out at their houses. When I asked permission, the answer was "no." I'd ask why and Ginny would say, "Because, it's not necessary," or, "You went to someone else's house a few days ago."

We never fed the neighborhood kids. Everyone was sent home at supper time. Ginny planned and portioned out food each evening. There was not enough to share with anyone. Once, Ginny bought some cookies that were practically candy bars—chocolate macaroons I think. We had a babysitter – the teenager who lived next door. I overheard her talking to a friend on the phone about the cookie she was eating. The next day when Ginny demanded to know who ate the cookie, I ratted out the babysitter.

A few years later, when I became a babysitter at other homes, I would be told to help myself to whatever I wanted to eat while I stayed late. Some mothers even made a plate of brownies just for me. We didn't share food the way other people did.

I had a Shoop Shoop hula hoop, a jump rope and from age of ten on, and I was the right weight to make the pogo stick work. I was never bored except in school. Teachers wrote observations in the permanent records that only other teachers and school personnel could see. The permanent records could be kept secret until the Sunshine Laws regarding school records passed in 1974. I turned eighteen in 1975 and found out I could demand to see my permanent record.

My elementary school teachers wrote in my permanent record that I was creative and bright but disorganized and not consistent about finishing homework. Some of them wrote about how I talked too much and spent too much time looking out of the window. Today, we medicate kids like that. I was unlucky when I reached fifth grade. There were two teachers for each level, and I got the one with the reputation for being the meanest teacher in school.

Mrs. Brimacomb probably should have gone into some profession other than teaching. She was an elegant middle-aged woman who dressed as if she belonged in an executive office. She was thin with a long neck and a short bouffant hairstyle. Her long neck with prominent tendons and her grumpy disposition lead to the nickname, "The Grinch."

I was on my own when it came to taking care of myself and any problems I had. I was expected to help out around the house as directed. I watched my little brother and set the table before dinner. I cleaned up after the evening meal and helped Eileen bake deserts from box mixes.

The school dress code still required girls to wear skirts or dresses and knee socks to school (even when the weather was freezing). I was on my way home from school one day after more than a foot of snow had fallen. Then freezing rain covered that snow with about a half inch of ice. I was very proud of the boots I was wearing, the kind you wore with only socks – no shoes underneath. They were almost knee high, made from fake leather and lined with fake fur.

As we left the school building, kids were sliding down the slope on the school grounds. The ice coating on top of the snow was very slick. It looked like fun. I decided to take a ride down the schoolyard hill before walking home. I slid standing, in my almost knee-high boots. Wheee! Then, near the bottom, there was a lot of broken ice with jagged edges sticking up over the deep soft snow beneath. I tripped on it, went down, and my knee was sliced open by a shard of ice.

I didn't feel it. If you must be cut open, an ice blade is the material most likely to cut through skin with no sensation at all. I noticed the gash on the front of my right knee because of the blood. But it didn't hurt. The cold probably numbed it. So I walked home, blood trickling down the front of my leg all the way. By the time I got there, the fake fur inside my boot was soaked with blood. I think that my mother bandaged my knee and rinsed out my boot.

Life went on. Because the gash was in a place where the flesh stretched as my knee bent, it would not heal very well. It might scab up while I slept, but when I sat at a desk in school the next day, it would open up and bleed. It might form a scab again by lunchtime, and then become itchy as the school day wore on.

I remember Mrs. Brimacomb interrupting a lesson and bellowing at me "leave that scab alone!" I don't recall getting any medical attention. I still have a scar on my knee. If I had a similar injury today, I would get stitches. If I saw someone with a similar gash, I would take them to an emergency room.

Mrs. Brimacomb also kept telling me "Stop scratching your head." I couldn't help it; my head was itchy. When I scratched the top of my head, I often found these little yellow things stuck to my scalp. I pulled them off hair shafts that they seemed to be glued on and looked at them. The hair often came out with them. I pressed them between my thumbnails, and they popped. Sticky goo would come out. I got an odd satisfaction finding and destroying these things. I never thought to ask anyone what they were. Sometimes I would see a bug that looked like a little black flea. If I caught one, I would crush it between my fingernails too.

I would learn many years later that I was nitpicking lice eggs and the occasional louse while my teacher and parents were scolding me for scratching my head and playing with my hair. Nobody ever thought to check my scalp for lice. I must have been pretty good at removing them because our house never got infested with lice and I eventually stopped finding bugs and their sticky eggs on my scalp. This may have what started me with obsessive hair pulling, leading to noticeable patches of missing hair. Until I was able to control the problem, I parted my hair on one side and swept it over the top to cover the scabby balding patches and kept this problem to myself.

Mrs. Brimacomb favored the prissiest girly-girls in the class. She obviously disliked boys, finding reasons to lecture them and take away privileges. Her greatest contempt she reserved for me and Laurie, the other tomboyish girl. After she finished yelling at the boys, she would single out me or Laurie for individual lectures. Not for anything we did wrong, but just for being wrong in general. Mrs. Brimacomb would lecture until a child cried, then move onto another. I learned to keep my tears from falling in her class. Eventually, I was able to sit there stone-faced while being lectured and wait until Mrs. Brimacomb gave up on me.

Looking back, I think she may have been having a mid-life crisis. She might have been happy in some other career but the social constructs of the time limited her career options as a woman. Mrs. Brimacomb had a daughter, an only child named Mitzi, who was in the fourth grade. When it came time for the combined fifth-grade classes to present a musical tribute to the history of the United States, Mitzi was allowed to perform the hula, representing Hawaii becoming a state, with the fifth-grade girls from her dance lessons.

I didn't take dance lessons, so I was not invited to shimmy in a grass skirt with Mitzi. I got to dress like a slave in rags and sing Negro spirituals with Juanita James, whose family had moved to the neighborhood the previous year. They were the second Black family in Tariffville. I was barely aware that an unusual number of people sold their houses the year the James family moved in. My parents later told me about the stupid bigots who believed their property values would drop because a second Black family had bought one of the houses in the development. I was fascinated by Juanita. She was so exotic, wearing a variety of hairstyles that defied gravity and entranced me as beautiful works of art.

Juanita sang the lead on "Swing Low Sweet Chariot," with Laurie and me singing back up, dressed in rags and straw hats and bare feet, in front of all the fifth-grade parents. I have to wonder how Juanita's parents felt. They had made it out of the city, only to have their beautiful daughter dressed like a slave and singing negro spirituals with the two scruffiest girls in the class.

At least they gave her the solo. I recall being quite happy to be comfortably dressed and barefoot in school. I loved singing with the most beautiful and exotic girl. I suspect Mrs. Brimacomb didn't believe she had provided me with anything to be proud of, but this was my happiest memory of fifth grade. Because our cohort of baby-boomers was too big for our local elementary school, we would be bused to the middle school in Simsbury starting in sixth grade.

Us and Them

Jack was frustrated and unhappy in the corporate world, so he created his own corporation with his own rules. He relished being his own boss. He considered himself and other independent business owners superior to the corporate drones who slowly worked their way up by persistence and luck. He chose to make his own life and demonstrated that this way was better. He had time to play with his kids and swim in the pool that he was able to build on the cheap because he decided when and how much time he could take off from work.

Ginny supported this view and told us that our teachers were not to be trusted because they had government jobs and therefore did not know anything about the real world of commerce, money, and politics. When she perused one of the newspapers or magazines over breakfast and found an article about how the majority of successful businessmen were Republicans, Jack changed parties.

Jack had been a Democrat. He admired John F. Kennedy, perhaps in part, due to their shared ethnic heritage and similar appearance. Jack may have also been influenced by the more Democratic ideals by his college experience and the GI Bill that provided for it. He seemed to have a sense of community that came with being an extrovert and having spent time in large organizations like the Navy, the YMCA, and sports teams. He witnessed and experienced the effects of social programs, unions, and communities more than Ginny did.

She was more of a loner and introvert, who was increasingly unnerved by news about crime, drugs, and the social disorder created by the unpopular Vietnam war and the resulting protests. Jack and Ginny were united by memories of World War II and the heroism and unity of the American good guys who saved the world by working together. It was wrong to question the government when it came to war and getting tough on crime, but it was okay to ridicule the bleeding heart leftists in Congress who wanted to help the poor and spend their taxes on education and social programs.

They gathered information and ideas like ammunition, about why they were right, and the left was wrong. They did this while choosing to live where the best public schools educated their children. They nursed resentment for people who had it easy with cushy government jobs that allowed them to do very little work all day while collecting good pay and benefits. They considered themselves smarter and more deserving because they struggled in the real world of competition and risk.

I straddled the conflicting messages about my parents versus the rest of the world when I saw teachers who showed up early in the morning and worked all day away from home. If I was visiting a friend whose father worked at a job instead of owning a business, I noticed that he left earlier and came home later than my father did. Ginny often had time to read the papers over coffee in the morning, and have a cocktail with the late afternoon talk shows before starting dinner.

In some ways, my parents were always at work, because they discussed business over the dinner and breakfast table, but they were usually at home and had control over their hours. I'm sure they felt more stressed than people with jobs, because of their need to push themselves, and the constant worry of uncertain income. This may have contributed to their solidifying belief that everything wrong with the country was the fault of their enemies on the left. When they had business setbacks, it was due to the influence of the left.

Their position seemed valid, in a way. The Vietnam war was increasingly unpopular and looking more and more like a mistake. Protests were affecting the way people voted, and the power was shifting. Slowing down, and eventually ending the war caused tremendous loss to the defense industry, it seemed. Our pretty hillside villages and quaint riverside towns were supported by munitions, explosives, and submarines. When the money stopped flowing, the small businesses that fed off the largesse of the killing machines began to wither and die. Soon the personnel business could not support the Hogan family, and Jack went looking for a job.

He was a poor fit for the few professional jobs he applied for and hated the idea of no longer being his own boss. Although he had the connections and the knowledge of how to get a corporate job, and after being in the very business of helping other people do just that, he struggled to find anything suitable in the shrinking economy. So, he went to night school and learned to be a realtor. Soon Hogan Real Estate was a reality. They had some yard signs printed up with green lettering on a white background: Hogan Real Estate with a leprechaun logo in case anyone didn't realize that Hogan was an Irish name and the new phone number.

Now the avocado-colored phone in the kitchen had a glowing white knob that needed to be twisted to answer the Real Estate line or the Personnel Search Associates line, which still rang occasionally. I had answered the business phones as needed from age twelve. When another phone line was added, my job as live-in answering service became more complicated.

A Bigger Boat

After fixing up one twenty-eight foot wooden boat up and selling it for a little more than he paid for it, Jack got a bigger boat: a thirty-two foot Chris-Craft with a lap-streak hull. He got it cheap because it, too, was made of wood. Wooden boats were prone to rotting and in need of annual scraping and painting, unlike the newer fiberglass boats. The cabin was arranged similarly to the former one, but it had more deck room out back. In addition to the narrow, cramped bunks, there was a bathroom the size of a small closet and a cooking area approximately two feet wide. It had a tiny sink and a two-burner stove.

We spent weekends on that Chris-Craft for a few years, keeping it in the cheapest, crappiest boatyard. (Classier places were called marinas.) When engine trouble or some other issue stranded it in the boatyard we stayed anyway; there were plenty of things for kids to do. I played with stray cats that hung around for the fishermen who cleaned fish and threw fish guts on the ground.

Danny and I learned to catch little green crabs and sold them to the bait shop. First, we tied smashed mussels to strings as bait, and then lowered them into the shallow water from the pier. When a crab climbed onto the bait and began nibbling, we slowly pulled the string and then shook the crab off into an old coffee can. We spent the money we got from the bait shop on candy. After a while, we purchased a crab trap, baited it with fish guts, and set the trap to catch crabs while we were away visiting beaches or seaports. Sometimes we threw fish guts at each other.

Salt air and sea breezes remind me of vacations and visit with relatives. I enjoyed the boating phase of our lives. It continued only a few years after my little brother was born. While his tracheotomy made sleeping difficult for him, something about being strapped to the seat on a rocking boat made him sleep better than at home in a motionless crib. Maybe it was the salty sea air, the motion of the waves, or perhaps it was the relaxed, happy atmosphere, but Timmy slept more soundly on the boat than at home.

For most people, boating is an extravagant form of recreation, but my parents found ways to make it affordable. We brought food and Ginny cooked it in the little galley. Sometimes we caught fish or dug clams, ate them and saved on food. We slept on board. Power boats are gas guzzlers, but during the time we were boating gas was about thirty cents per gallon. Compared to motel rentals and restaurant food, our boating vacations rivaled camping on the affordability scale. If things went well, the boat could even be sold at a profit after we had done all the maintenance ourselves.

Jack might have been able to get back some of the money he put into the Chris-Craft if he had taken proper care of its two engines. These motors were the same as the kind used in pick-up trucks. But instead of being cooled with radiators full of anti-freeze conditioned water, these engines used water pumped up from wherever the boat happened to be. For this boat, that usually meant salt water. I later learned that if the salty water is not drained out each year when the boat is stored for the winter, it corrodes the engine blocks. Jack probably did not realize this.

Near the middle of the last season we had that boat, both engines broke. Saltwater and crank-case oil mixed into gunky, grey goo as thick as chocolate pudding. We still went to the boatyard each weekend, but instead of going places we stayed in the boatyard while my father and one of his friends tried in vain to salvage the engines. He ended up selling it at a loss. Jack's belief—that by being resourceful and clever he could have what rich people had, on the cheap—didn't always work.

Autism III

Autism was not listed in the earliest editions of the Diagnostic and Statistical Manuals DSM-I, DSM-II). What they did list were Childhood Schizophrenia and Mental Retardation. These were the only classifications into which a child (who might later be labeled Autistic) could be placed by a pediatrician, psychiatrist or psychologist. So, Autistic children of the 50s and 60s would be assumed to be suffering from Mental Retardation or Childhood Schizophrenia.

Childhood Schizophrenia is not listed in the DSM-5. Schizophrenia is typically an illness that becomes apparent in the late teens or early adulthood, Autism is typically seen in children before the age of two. Some Autistic children show signs of the disorder as infants and others develop typically and have a slow or dramatic regression by age two with the loss of previously developed social and language skills.

Rett Syndrome is still listed in the DSM-5 and is indicated as a rare condition more typical in girls who develop typically up to age four and then suddenly or gradually show signs of Autism; it was previously called Childhood Disintegrative Syndrome. Many people are not recognized as having

Autism until they become teens or even adults. Gathering information about their early development is difficult. Sometimes there was clear evidence that the characteristics of Autism were apparent much earlier, but not recognized or diagnosed. Some children were seen as having unusual behavior and developmental delays that were noticed and documented by parents. These problems were monitored and later diagnosed as Autism. Some parents report that symptoms were not apparent and saw normal development through the early years.

Collecting accurate retrospective data on children and adults with Autism about their earliest years is problematic. Babies and toddlers are usually assessed by questioning caregivers and parents. If a parent is asked about concerns they had about their child's early behavior, they may have difficulty recalling precise sequences of memories or recall things that fit leading questions that doctors or psychologists ask them about their child. Parents can also fail to notice delays and problems in firstborn or only children.

PUSSY WILLOW

Pussy, wooly pussy willow

I love you in the Spring!

When Autumn leaves start to fall

You will have gone your time

For the Autumn mists, the world will change

Springtime is your weather still

Pussy willow glow and glow and glow

-Eileen

Chapter 5
The Enemy

Guitar Lessons

My parents purchased a business property on Hopmeadow Street that had office space and room for little retail shops. They rented the shops to tenants and reserved an office for their own business. It was more professional than the basement office at home. Ginny still worked in the basement office, but Jack met with clients at what we called "The Building."

At age twelve, I picked up a cheap guitar that had been given to Danny for Christmas one year. He was expected to teach himself to play from a book. He never learned to play it. There were group guitar lessons offered a few miles away for the low price of $10.00 for ten lessons; I had saved that much from babysitting. I had been trying to teach myself to play Danny's guitar, and I asked to be taken to guitar lessons. The class was near The Building, so Ginny could drop me off for my weekly guitar class, and then go on to The Building to vacuum and clean.

I learned the basics, practicing until I could change chords without breaking the rhythm. In class, the teacher would have everyone form a G chord with their left hand. She demonstrated the strum pattern saying, "Down, down-up, down" then shouted "change to C!" She then paused while everyone re-arranged their left hands, then resumed, "down, down-up, down." I changed chords quickly and strummed through her pauses. I had plenty of time to practice. I learned to play songs by Joan Baez, the Beatles, Peter Paul and Mary, Bob Dylan, and Simon and Garfunkel. I played in my room. Jack had built an addition over the garage at the far end of the house for us three older kids.

My parents recommended I learn songs that didn't require singing because I sang wrong. My friends liked my singing, but my parents told me I needed voice lessons. I couldn't afford voice lessons, so I kept my singing to myself. I took comfort in the realization that they hated the way all the popular female singers that I loved sang as much as they hated my voice.

Middle School

By seventh grade, I was often miserable in school. I was even more miserable at home, so I rarely stayed home sick. I didn't fit in. I got picked on as I grew to my full adult height. I was only permitted to take a bath once a week and puberty had made me smelly. My classmates noticed and humiliated me about it.

There were some empathic teachers in the Simsbury school system. Sometimes one would notice I was troubled and attempt to help me with kind words and encouragement. "What is wrong?" "Let me help you." My reaction to their kindness was to feel a lump in my throat that made it hard to speak. It was those "feelings" again. My eyes would burn with the tears I was too proud to spill. I was unable to react appropriately to the help they offered. Their kindness had the opposite effect, left me feeling raw and depressed.

The home economics teacher was an older lady named Mrs. Lampkin. She was called "Lammy-Pie" behind her back because she was so kind, sweet, and grandmotherly. I nearly flunked home economics, although my sewing projects came out better than most. Boys were segregated in industrial arts class at the time, so they did some extra girls-only lessons for us in home economics.

There was one project that was almost too painful for me to do. We were to read and write about how to dress and wear our hair in the most flattering ways. We were to describe our beauty assets and liabilities, and then describe the best kind of clothes and hairstyle to make the most of our assets and conceal our flaws. We were expected to include pictures of ourselves and images cut from magazines. We were also supposed to write about our hygiene routines.

It was torture for me to do this assignment. I had no control over my hairstyle, bathing schedule, or clothing choices. I had very little self-esteem and could not bear to write about my round face, short forehead, and gangly, under-developed figure. Most of my clothes did not fit properly due to my growth spurt. I was bigger than both of my older siblings and felt like I was huge and overweight.

When Mrs. Lampkin gently tried to help me finish my report, I stiffened up and became uncooperative. I handed in an incomplete, sloppy, project with no pictures. I had an A on my sewing project, but my style report brought my final grade down to a D. I got lots of Ds in middle school. My parents punished me by taking away the guitar lessons. I continued to play and teach myself how to do finger-picking techniques and chords from books and listening to the radio.

My parent's habits of punishing me with swats and ridicule for complaining or crying, along with Mrs. Brimacomb's cruelty, had made it difficult for me to admit to needing any help or accepting any help that was offered. In high school, I took an advanced tailoring class. The teacher told me that while I was good at sewing and figuring out how to construct clothes, I worked too independently. I couldn't understand why this was a problem. Wasn't it good that I didn't bother her if I could figure things out by myself?

A Job!

My best friend Nancy suggested we look for work one warm spring day when we were in seventh grade. Nancy was a bold, free-range girl being raised by her father and his much-younger girlfriend. Her mother had left the family when she got pregnant with the man she was having an affair with and then married. Nancy got the idea that there was work at one of the two churches. We went to the Catholic Church, knocked on the rectory door, and Nancy asked if there was anything we could do to earn some money. Father Shae said that there was. Next thing I knew Nancy and I were clipping grass around the headstones in the cemetery with hand clippers. The kind of string trimmers commonly called weed-whackers hadn't yet been invented.

Two creepy men mowed the graveyard all spring and summer, along with digging graves as needed. Trimming all the grass around the heads stones was more than they could accomplish. We trimmed for Memorial Day, Independence Day and Labor Day. Nancy and I had a job a few days work each summer, and Father Shae would write us checks for twenty dollars each for a day's work. We were supplied bandages when blisters arose. I had to fight off the groping of one of the gravediggers who was eighteen and wanted to be my boyfriend. He lost that idea after I kicked him. I kicked him so hard I nearly knocked his legs out from under him. I was aiming for his crotch, but he turned defensively and took it on the thigh. I bet there was a nasty bruise.

Nancy and I were excited to get paid regularly, and we learned a lot about local history by reading the names and ages on the headstones. We learned that many families were completely wiped out by illnesses. We saw that boys only a year or two older than us died as soldiers in the Civil War. We learned about the connections to the earliest settlers of our village and could trace our classmates back nearly 300 years.

We brought bagged lunches and ate them sitting on top of gravestones. An elderly visitor was upset to find two sweaty girls in short pants sitting on the tombstones when she came to visit. Jack bragged that his daughter had a job with hundreds of people under her. He once had the same job when he was a kid. Nancy and I worked after school and sometimes all day that summer, clipping grass before Independence Day and Labor Day. I recall getting that check for $20 and was so excited when I rode my bike home.

Having this job meant I could hang around with my best friend all day. My mother didn't object to me being away from home all day. She even provided many band-aids for the blisters that we acquired from the constant clipping. Nancy and I started ninth grade together, but that spring she went to live with her mother.

Private Thoughts

One afternoon when I was thirteen and had just started eighth grade, I was sitting alone in my room when I was summoned to the basement office by Ginny. Jack was there too. This was not a good sign. I was in deep trouble.

I sat down in the faux leather side chair they kept for interviewing clients. There was a short period of silence while I wondered what it was I had done this time. They showed me a piece of notebook paper that looked like it had been folded up and then unfolded. I realized it was the note I had written to my future self two years ago. The letter I hoped would remind me that if I had any children, I would encourage them to talk about their feelings and that I should try to understand them. I had forgotten all about it. Now I was filled with dread.

"Why would you write such a thing?" Jack furiously demanded, speaking for both of them. They lectured, belittled, shamed and humiliated me for daring to think and write down such self-pitying nonsense. They demanded I apologize and never do anything like that again. They told me I should never write down any angry thoughts. They told me they were going to keep the letter as an example of what kind of child I was.

I was confused and hurt. My parents were free to express their anger in any way they wanted. They could rant about people at town hall meetings who disapproved of the building renovations or zoning changes they requested. They could rage about politicians and celebrities. They could cuss and fume about the god-damned hippie freak communists who were protesting the Vietnam War, or the liberals who were ruining the country. They could say, "America, love it or leave it!" when war protests and anti-war journalists and politicians were featured on the evening news or some talk show. I was not permitted to complain, or even write down my feelings in private.

The ranch house was crowded. Timmy was getting too big to stay in a crib in the same room as our parents. Jack built an addition over the garage area where he previously enclosed the carport. Another garage was added on, and the original carport would soon hold the stairway to the second floor and a kitchen expansion. Jack added three bedrooms, one for each of us older kids and a sitting room where we could watch television and not bother the adults about the shows we wanted to watch. Danny, Eileen, and I each got a room of our own, and Timmy moved into Danny's old room sleeping on the bed with broken springs from our bed-jumping days. He later told me he could sleep anywhere because he grew up sleeping with broken springs poking him all night.

The room I had shared with Eileen became a guest room. We divided the sock and underwear that we had shared and organized our own things in our own dressers. The new furniture was scavenged from leftover donations to the Chamber of Commerce Charity Auction Jack volunteered to manage. The addition was great. I had the Southwest corner room, and it was perfect if a bit hot in the summer. There was no bathroom upstairs and once when I was nauseous I knew I couldn't make it down the stairs, through the kitchen, and past the dining room to the bathroom, so I just puked out the window.

We could retreat from the evening news and avoid the Vietnam War body counts and news of the protests that always seemed to make Jack and Ginny angry. Eileen could disappear quietly into her room and do her arts and crafts. Danny and I could stay up late watching an early rock and roll variety show called Midnight Special. We saw the first seasons of Saturday Night Live. Our TV was black and white so we would watch things that everyone enjoyed in the old living room. We all watched Laugh-In, The Glenn Campbell Good Time Hour, and Sonny and Cher downstairs. We also watched the Smothers' Brothers Comedy hour until Jack and

Ginny found their liberal humor too irritating. We could go upstairs and watch them in black and white.

The Enemy

Sometimes my father would playfully hit me. When I asked why he'd say "That's for next time." He did it as a joke, but this joke had a cruel back-story. When Ginny was in high school, her father heard and believed a rumor about her being promiscuous. He refused to speak to her for a year. When Ginny found out why he wasn't speaking to her, she gathered evidence and supporters to prove her innocence. Although her father accepted the facts she presented, he refused to apologize for the unwarranted punishment and told her, "That's for next time."

Guilty until proven innocent seems to be the attitude my parents took when there was doubt regarding wrongdoing on the part of us children. Punishments mistakenly meted out would serve to cover future misdeeds or those that went undiscovered. (My husband informs me this was very much the attitude taken by the nuns at his school.) Humanistic ideas had not yet supplanted typical parenting at that time, which connected to the puritanical belief that children were evil and in need of civilizing. Authoritarianism was the norm.

The daily body counts of American soldiers in Vietnam and war protests over the draft would lead to World War II being retrospectively called "the Good War." Veterans of the Good War ran the country. (Every president from Truman through Carter served in combat). Our leaders fervently believed we were the good guys who could fix the world's problems with our military might. In my parents' generational view, our country went to war when enemies attacked. For them, there was no practical difference between WWII and Vietnam: when America called you, you obediently and enthusiastically joined your classmates and friends (and in Jack's case, your older brother) and went off to fight.

For some reason the war in Vietnam has not been casually referred to as "the Bad War," but bad it was. My generation grew up with more literature, more education, and more prosperity than our parents had. We had the time to read, the luxury of thought, and the compulsion to question. We saw a clear distinction. The Good War sent men and boys aged seventeen through forty-five off to battle aggression by forces that, reviewed after the fact, were undeniably evil, brutal and vicious. The Vietnam conflict sent young men aged eighteen through twenty-nine, many of whom were too young to vote, off to prevent the spread of an idea. Many believed the former war was worth dying for, but the current war effort was not supported by a unified majority.

The "generation gap" widened the disparity between the postwar generation and mine. A significant factor was birth control pills, which became available in 1960. Sex could be separated from reproduction. A sexual revolution took place, lasting until the AIDS epidemic of the 1980s. Civil rights marches and the woman's liberation movement added to the cacophony of the anti-war protest. The hippie movement colored my youth with psychedelic patterns on clothes, folk and rock music, and creative expression of all kinds.

At the dinner table once when I was in eighth grade, I shared something I had read about the how India was attempting to reduce the population growth by offering men money or transistor radios in exchange for submitting to vasectomies. From the time I was able to read the newspapers and magazines that flowed into our house, I reported at the dinner table on what I found interesting.

As Ginny was questioning my veracity, the phone rang, and my father left the table to answer it. We always answered the phone even during dinner because it might be a business call. There were separate lines for home and business phones, but in 1969 they both had the same ringtone. My father returned to the dining room gleefully announcing, "It's for Sharon, and it's a boy!" Then, to me, he said: "Ask him if he has a transistor radio."

That was embarrassing enough, but what happened next was even more embarrassing. I went to take the call. It was one of my classmates, and he was sincerely interested in talking to me. All I could think was that he was probably sitting there surrounded by friends while he played a cruel joke on the ugly girl. I was rude to him and hung up. I'm sorry now. He deserved my attention, and I might have liked him. We might have been a couple and developed some fond memories.

There were still some laughs and fun times at home, but I became a depressed, under-achieving sullen adolescent. My parents were increasingly irritated by my complaints and my failure to behave as they expected.

I was growing so fast my clothes didn't fit. I felt that my arms and legs were too long, rather than thinking that the sleeves and pants were too short. If something was too tight, it was because I was too fat. I thought I should weigh less than Eileen, who was slightly built. She was older by two years and had stopped getting taller when she had reached five foot five at age thirteen. I grew to almost five foot eight by age thirteen, and my older sister was wearing the clothes that no longer fit me. I could no longer wear hand-me-downs from Eileen like I did when I was younger. Danny was so skinny that I could only wear his outgrown shoes.

Just as my hips were developing, jeans and slacks for girls were made to ride low on those hips. Hip-hugger pants were all that we could find on the clearance racks of the close-out stores where we got most of my middle and high school clothes. Jack would comment that my ass looked like I was smuggling watermelons in my jeans when I wore the kind of clothes that were popular in the late 60s and early 70s. As my weight inched up past 100, then 110, then reached 120 pounds, I felt fat and ugly.

My parents often told me that we don't air our dirty laundry in public. With both of my brothers having medical problems and my sister's condition on top of that, I was not permitted the indulgence of having my own troubles, which were considered petty by comparison. I was often lectured by my father about being their only normal child, but the one who caused more trouble than the others. My parents forgave my brothers and sister for the problems they had. They had medical and psychiatric problems. I had no excuse.

My problems might be considered typical issues to be expected of growing children. I sometimes broke the rules. I wanted to dress and act like my friends. I questioned the demands my parents made of me to look and think as they expected me to. I dared to challenge their authority. In most families, this made me an average kid. In my family, it made me a traitor, a trouble-maker, a problem child with no cause to have any problems at all.

People may have wondered what I had to be depressed or irritated about, besides puberty and the awkwardness of growing taller sooner than most girls. In addition to being expected to be untroubled, I was supposed to sit still several times each year while my mother cut my hair. I couldn't experiment with variations like ponytails or braids. There was only one way that my mother permitted me to wear my hair until I was fourteen. She was able to do a relatively professional job of cutting men's hair. She gave my Father neat haircuts and used the clippers to give my brother Danny crew cuts for many years after they were no longer fashionable for boys.

From the time I was three years old to age fourteen; I was given a short page-boy cut, almost identical to my sister's. We looked like Scout Finch in "To Kill a Mockingbird." To reduce the number of haircuts needed, our bangs were cut very short and sometimes unevenly. As the 1960s passed by, short hair was out. I began more and more to hate the haircut she gave me. Another effect of puberty was that my hair grew kinky in a few places. I got into the habit of finding the wiry hairs and yanking them out.

Hair

Although I was often grounded because of poor school performance or some other indiscretion, this usually meant I couldn't go to places that required being driven, or to a friend's house. I was generally free to go for long walks if I wasn't needed to babysit or answer the business phones.

I liked hiking the hills and natural land nearby, ranging a couple of miles in any direction. There was the slow-moving part of the river to the west with a floodplain area, with footpaths I could wander on. Laurel Hill to the east was called "The Mountain" by the local kids. There were woodsy trails and views from the top of the hill. If I were particularly upset, I would head north to the Gorge. At the Gorge, the

Farmington River became boiling current of rapids that curved around the north end of town and squeezed through the natural cut in Laurel Hill, and a broken dam that pushed the whole river into a powerful, churning, spout. I would cut through the brambles and avoid the poison ivy to get close to the rushing water. I imagined the water pulling away my roiling emotions, and washing them off to the sea. Meditative walks in nature became a life-long habit.

Hair was a significant issue at our house. To my parents, long, loose, natural hairstyles were a sign of rebellion and social decay. The Broadway musical, "Hair" pretty much spelled out that long hair represented freedom and a general rejection of social norms and order that were held dear by conservative members of the older generation. Girls were wearing their hair as long as it would grow and boys were wearing their hair longer too.

The summer of 1970 must have involved too many distractions for my mother to give me the usual number of haircuts. By August, my hair was nearly shoulder length, and my bangs were long enough to clip to the side. I was looking forward to starting high school with a new look. I was beginning to look almost normal in the mirror. I was looking forward to a fresh start in high school with new classes. Perhaps there would be less exposure to bullies. I was hoping to blend in and maybe make some new friends.

Three days before I started high school, my mother sat me down for the haircut. I think she made it even shorter than usual, to make up for the extra growth. Puberty usually makes girl's hair grow faster. In my case, the hair not only grew faster, but it also became more wavy and textured. It was horrible. When it was over, I saw in the mirror an awkward girl with short choppy bangs with a style that was more than twenty years out of date. I cried for the rest of that day and all the next. Instead of starting high school with the confidence that I might fit in, I went slouching, red-eyed, and ashamed to be seen.

Ginny never said anything about the bad haircut. I never said anything directly to her about it. I assume she realized how distraught I was and stopped insisting on cutting my hair after that. My brother Danny benefited from my rebellion, and after my demonstration, Ginny no longer subjected him to the crew cut.

After that, I would be allowed to grow my hair long but had to put up with frequent insults from both my parents about how horrible it looked. My father threatened to cut my hair off while I slept. He regularly said that I looked like shit. He remarked that my head was like an explosion in a mattress factory. He told me he was so ashamed of the way I looked that I should change my name.

If I discussed a differing point of view over dinner, perhaps that the war in Vietnam wasn't a good idea, I was in for ridicule. If Jack got overly angry and loud, Ginny would say "Enough already stop it!" Jack was not immune to the hairy eyeball. Later, Jack would take me aside and say, "If there were a war in this country tomorrow, you and I would be on different sides."

I was a teenager and had no interested in fighting any war. I followed the news and listened to arguments for and against the Vietnam War. I was confused and afraid. I had questions, but discussing the issue with my parents was asking to be yelled at or hit. As I grew older and looked more like the kind of communist hippie that he believed was destroying his world, Jack was infuriated with me more frequently. When Ginny made him stop telling me at dinner that I was a piece of shit he would later say to me privately, "You're leaving this house before you ruin my marriage."

Ginny was concerned with how I presented myself outside the house. She would rudely insist, "Do something with your hair," before we went anywhere. I put it into a ponytail or threw on a scarf to hold my hair back or keep it down. I once used a chemical hair straightener from the drug store, bought with money I'd earned. My hair was a smooth and straight as that of a Native American Princess. I looked like someone else for a few days. After I washed it, the damage was apparent. The formerly slick, smooth hairs split and became dry, damaged, and nearly as frizzy as before the treatment. For all the insults and demands that I "do something" about my hair, I never saw a hairdresser or had any help from them finding products that might make my appearance more acceptable.

In addition to having unruly hair that seemed to insist on a life of its own, my body changed and developed like any young woman's. The acne, the curves, and irregular cycles made me wish I was tiny or invisible. I tried to actually become smaller and less visible. I slouched so much that standing up straight for any reason became difficult. I developed body dismorphic disorder and avoided mirrors. I skipped lunch at school, dieted and often secretly binged on the cakes, candy, and cookies that were usually available to stretch the food budget and keep my skinny siblings from looking like they weren't fed.

Jack and Ginny considered themselves sophisticated and certainly indulged in the kind of drinking that was common at the time. Jack had been exposed to marijuana by way of some of the jazz musicians he had associated with when he was in college, but he had avoided it. Neither of them smoked cigarettes or approved of any of the values presented by the changing culture of the beatniks, hippies, and war protesters. They seemed threatened by the freedom and ideas. Perhaps they associated the folk music and sexual revolution with communism and disrespect for the country.

Once, Jack was ranting at dinner about all the drug use and pot smoking that the god-damned hippie freaks were doing. Danny and I had received a thorough education in health class regarding all these dangerous substances, how they would drive you to addiction and madness. We were well informed about drugs although the drug training was so over-the-top exaggerated that we took much of it with a grain of salt. But we were taught about the effects of alcohol along with all the scary tales of drug use. We compared pot smoking to the evening cocktails Ginny and Jack consumed regularly.

Jack insisted that alcohol was not a drug because it was legal, ancient, and used in church ceremonies. We showed him the dictionary and encyclopedia pages refuting his position, but he never backed down. It didn't get ugly or personal I think, because Danny was involved in this particular debate. They didn't see him as an enemy or symbol of what was wrong with the world.

WWII had colored my parents' youth with unity and patriotism which they associated with being righteous and brave. The stress of trying to make enough money to pay the bills and the social and economic changes they believed created business challenges made them irritable. Jack, in particular, found it easy to blame all the stress and misfortune on the evils of those who dared up-end the status quo. There I sat at his table with my long and shaggy hair. I became a slouching, depressed, and unkempt representation of all the things that were ruining the world his generation had built. I was the enemy, the disloyal one, a perfect scapegoat for his frustration and rage.

Church or the Library

As I was questioning and exploring the world of ideas, lifestyles, and beliefs, young people throughout the country were forming communes. Psychedelic drugs were a new way to expand your mind. My family had stopped going to church shortly after my little brother came. I briefly attended our local Catholic Church on my own for a few months at age fourteen. They even had me playing guitar in the folk mass for a while. I almost had to quit that gig because some old biddy in the congregation thought that my long legs—which had recently outgrown most of my appropriate-for-church dresses and skirts—did not belong up near the altar.

This gentle old priest offered to buy me a longer dress or skirt. My parents were offended by this charitable offer. They refused it. I went to the basement and found some fabric in the basement stash, and using skills learned in home economics; I sewed myself a nice, appropriately knee-length dress.

I played at the folk mass once or twice after that, but the sermons were not making sense to me. As much as I enjoyed playing folk music at the front of the congregation, I had realized that I was not a Catholic and didn't believe what the priest was saying in his sermons.

Astrology was popular, and many of my schoolmates took astrologer's advice and interpretations of the zodiac signs seriously. I read up on Astrology but didn't find the answers and certainty I was looking for.

In high school, science was my favorite subject, and I had been reading about psychology. While I often was refused permission to leave the house to visit friends or participate in activities, I would always be permitted to go to work. I began babysitting around the neighborhood at age eleven or twelve. I was often asked to babysit for other families in the neighborhood and was often paid a dollar per hour. Those neighbors provided me with cookies or welcomed me to help myself in the fridge. Alone, with the sleeping children, I would read books and was considered an excellent sitter.

Once, a little girl I was babysitting got frightened by a shadow that was on her bedroom wall at night. I had no idea what she was calling it as she was cowering in her bed saying she was afraid of, "maninahat." I suggested that she say "Boo!" She said she was too frightened so I offered to scare it away for her. I jumped around the room waving my arms and saying, "Booga, booga, booga!" She giggled and went to sleep. Her mother later informed me that the shadow of the curtain and its rod against the wall looked like a man in a hat; therefore, "maninahat."

When I reported to a babysitting job with a fat book that contained a biography of Sigmund Freud, my employers were impressed. I learned more about science and found more meaning and satisfaction in learning about psychology.

The occult, witchcraft, and eastern religions I had been reading about held less attraction as I learned more science. I kept an open mind about hidden powers and unexplained phenomena. I read up on herbs and wild plants with medicinal and nutritive value. There was a fine line between the science, the folklore and the magical claims regarding plant life. I studied fortune-telling techniques. By the time I transitioned from high school to college, I had realized fortune telling was the art of using props and intuition, quickly evaluating available information and making informed guesses that gave the illusion of knowing things through supernatural power.

I was an eccentric kid. My reading and experimenting was tolerated and sometimes nurtured. Ginny was a frustrated artist who had enjoyed being a student. She often spoke about the things she enjoyed learning about in college. After getting married, having twice as many children as she wanted and being a business partner, she had little time to read or study. I was encouraged to learn about and explore ideas of all sorts. Because we lived in a tiny village surrounded by undeveloped land and there was no public transportation, I had plenty of time to study the natural world and develop hobbies like yoga and herbalism. I was not involved with sports or after-school activities, so, my life outside school was relatively unstructured.

After my abysmal middle school performance, I was placed in track three when I started high school. They put the best students in track one, average students in track two, and the ones who had trouble passing classes in track three. My high school freshman English class was full of juniors and seniors retaking freshman English for a third or fourth time so they could graduate.

We weren't expected to read much in track three. We read magazine and articles and discussed TV commercials. I found the reading lists the track one kids had and read most of their books. I enjoyed reading "The Scarlet Letter" on my own. There was something about the outcast woman wearing her punishment with a kind of perverse pride that struck a chord in me. I admired Hester Prynne's fierce independence and creative rebellion. I was developing some fierce rebellious

116

pride in being from the wrong side of town, making my clothes instead of having them purchased for me, and taking long walks alone along the riverbanks and scenic hillsides surrounding my neighborhood instead of going out shopping with friends driving their own cars.

The art teacher allowed me to create an independent study class I called "Natural Textile Manufacturing." I ordered some raw wool and taught myself how to make yarn with a treadle sewing machine I had converted into a spindle. I dyed the wool using wild plants and onion peels. I found all the information I needed in library books.

I entered the ninth grade with Nancy. She was cooler and more socially outgoing than me, had charmed her way into a group of good-looking rich kids from the other side of town. I felt that I was only welcomed in this clique as Nancy's friend. At some point, my parents decided that Nancy's home was a bad influence and insisted that she come to our house rather than allowing me to go to hers. With a peace activist father and a younger live-in girlfriend helping to pay the bills, this was *enemy territory*.

Nancy's older sisters were beautiful, long-haired hippies. Her father was of Polish and Russian ancestry, and ethnically Jewish. He wrote anti-war (Vietnam) letters to the local paper which infuriated my parents. The whole family was atheist; Nancy told me how her grandfather ridiculed religion and believed that after one dies, one rots. I was intrigued by this idea and probably surprised that an adult would share this idea with a child. I already suspected that religion was a lie created by some powerful human authorities to compel children—and later adults—to behave properly out of fear. In my case, the adults in my family would not even hint that a divine ultimate authority was probably a lie. Nancy's cantankerous grandfather gave credence to my suspicions about the existence of God. I tucked this idea away, to consider more as I continued to learn about life and people.

Preppies and Townies

I met Sue in art class when I was a sophomore. My best friend Nancy had moved away, and Sue had fallen out with her best friend, Ellen sometime before we met. Art teachers allowed us to chat while we worked on projects and even let us come to the art room during our study hall periods if we worked on projects, helped the teacher with her work and behaved appropriately. Sue thought I was funny and giggled at my ideas and observations. This encouraged me to share more amusing and odd thoughts. I started a recognition ritual with Sue that we both found fun. If we saw each other in the hallway at school, we would begin walking in a zigzag pattern.

Soon Sue and I realized that we lived only a few miles away from each other and could meet at a park that was half-way between where each of us lived. We rode our bicycles to meet there. I was waiting in the park when I saw sue on her bike. I began walking in zigzags. Sue got off her bike and walked in zigzags as well.

I was under the impression that it was mostly bad children that were sent to Catholic school. I had only known about kids who were sent there to be 'straightened out' by nuns who were so good at discipline. Some of my public school classmates were sent off to Catholic school after falling in with the wrong crowd or becoming unmanageable at home. Sue lived on the other side of the River, which was considered the better side of town. I was surprised to learn that she had been sent to Catholic school from kindergarten through eighth grade. Her family had a tradition of sending their children to Catholic School.

Sue's mother was very religious, and they attended church regularly. I saw things at her house that were new to me. They lived in a big house, her older brothers were married men, and she had the option of inviting friends to stay overnight in her spacious bedroom. Sue had a brand-new beautiful gown to participate in a family wedding. She had new silk shoes dyed to match the dress. I had seen such things. My mother had some lovely gowns from her younger days tucked away in the basement. They were not purchased at high-end stores like Sue's because she sewed them herself.

Sue's bedroom had two beds so she could have friends stay over and talk all night. Her mother cooked more than enough food, and they ate family style, passing heaping bowls and plates around, and each person took as much or as little food as they liked. At my house, Mom divided the food and served each a portion. We were expected to eat everything on our plates. I usually ate quickly so I could leave the table. I went back later to clean up after everyone had finished. Sue's family meals were pleasant. There was no reason to leave early and everyone helped to clean up afterward.

One day in art class, Sue was crying over a letter she was holding. The letter was from Ellen, her former best friend wishing to resume being friends. Ellen was in Sue's class, and soon we became a threesome. Ellen lived on the campus of Westminster School, an all-boy's prep school where her father was a teacher. She was the youngest child of much older parents. Through her connection with Ellen, Sue got a job in the kitchen at the Westminster School. It had a huge campus that was set back from the road and hidden behind trees. My school bus passed it every day, and I was never aware of it until I began hanging around with Sue and Ellen.

Several expensive boarding schools in the area catered to the extremely wealthy. To the elite boys, at Westminster School, we were the townies. Our paths rarely crossed, but if we were aware of them, we knew them as the preppies. Some of the preppie boys built an A-frame cabin in the woods between their school and where Sue lived. She got to know some of them, and somehow parties were arranged to take place at Sue's house. The boys wanted to socialize with girls and came over. Sue invited me and any other local girls who were interested in coming. I brought my guitar and shared it with anyone who knew how to play.

At some point during these parties, we would all go for a walk in the woods. We went to the A-Frame and smoked so much pot the little shed became filled with smoke. We then walked back to Sue's house, ate snacks and tried not to giggle too much. I even snagged a preppie boyfriend who called me every day for a week and once invited me to hang out on the sprawling campus. Then he decided he didn't want to two-time his other townie girlfriend. I was beginning to think maybe I wasn't so ugly or fat.

Broken Things

I went to yoga classes offered as an alternative to study hall in school. Then I read every book I could find on the subject. The Maharishi Mahesh Yogi brought Transcendental Meditation to the United States. It cost $35 for students to get a personalized mantra and instructions on meditation that would change the student's life and make them better people. I read up on it and didn't want to waste $35, so I read up on meditation and taught myself how to meditate. A cousin of mine became a Jehovah's Witness and sent back all Christmas, birthday and other holiday cards to the rest of the family.

I harbored the secret desire from about the age of twelve that being a psychologist would be worth many years of school. It was even worth checking the spelling of my work if there was a chance I could learn how to help people like my sister and understand the kinds of problems I had. Being a below-average student made it sound ridiculous to say out loud that I wanted to be a psychologist, so I kept it to myself until my grades and SAT scores indicated I might be college material after all.

Being thrifty and finding ways to get something cheap or free was what I was brought up to do. I wanted to get into graduate school as quickly and inexpensively as possible, so when it came to getting my bachelor's degree, I went to the cheapest schools and took every shortcut I could find. For the most part, this bargain-hunting attitude worked in my favor, especially when it came to religious experiences. I never paid for a class when a book could provide the same information. I never paid for an experience that with some research and energy I could create for myself rather than having it spoon-fed to me by an expert. When I did pay for things, like college classes, I made sure I got my money's worth. I attended class, asked questions, and read all the assignments.

When I was fourteen, Jack took me to the garage of a friend of a friend who worked at the place that made Ovation Guitars. Ovation guitars were part traditional guitar, but with a curved fiberglass back that was designed to enhance the sound of the strings more beautifully than conventional guitars. A defense contractor called Kaman Aircraft had lost a contract to make helicopter blades for the Army. The owner used the woodworking, fiberglass, and computer design technology to create a new kind of guitar. Glen Campbell and Jim Croce played them. The factory that made them was near our home. If a guitar came out flawed and didn't pass inspection, it was spirited out of the factory and sold through word of mouth.

At that garage, I handed over all of my savings at the time: $40.00; and, we went home with a fantastic guitar whose only flaws were a cracked head and a discolored line in the middle of the soundboard. It sounded incredible. The neck was slender and the strings responsive to my touch. I curled around the trademark curved back and spent hours every day through my teens strumming, picking and howling. That guitar was my best non-human friend for decades.

Jack nearly doubled the size of our ranch house in Tariffville. (see picture page 17.) He had gradually added rooms, garages, and a second-floor suite. When he couldn't afford lumber, or the help of contractors, construction stopped until he had the money or found a deal. The old garage would eventually be made into an expanded eat-in kitchen and sun-room when enough money and time became available. If my father had a motto, it might have been, "If it ain't broke, it's too expensive."

My father may have been suffering from type 2 diabetes (adult-onset) at the time which would not be diagnosed unless it had caused a severe infection. I am told by people with diabetes that blood sugar fluctuation can make for some horrible mood swings. Jack may have not known that it was his body making him angry and took his anger out on me when he was suffering from low blood sugar.

My parents insisted that anger was only allowed to the adults in the house. Ginny was self-righteously angry much of the time, although she never had blood sugar problems. They would hit, kick, punch and slap me in anger for doing what they called "mouthing off." I was subjected to long tirades about being useless, an embarrassment to the family, a problem. I was often surprised by these physical attacks because they were not consistent. Sometimes I could talk, complain, or even disagree with them and just be told, "Enough!" or, "Because I said so." The hitting seemed random.

Jack once punched me in the kidney while I was working in the kitchen, over something I had said earlier, or for having a bad attitude. When I was an adult, he remembered that incident, and he thought it was funny or ironic. You see, I wore a watch band that was missing one of the tiny springs connecting it to the watch. I had attached the band to the watch by threading a straight pin through it and bending it over with pliers. The sharp end of the pin was folded over the top part of the watch band. It occasionally caught on my clothes, but it held my watch on. That day Jack punched me in the kidney, I recoiled, and the pin raked a gash up his forearm. He didn't say anything about it at the time.

Years later Jack liked to tell the story about how he wore long sleeves for weeks afterward so I wouldn't know that I had cut him. He joked that sometimes parents say, "This hurts me more than it hurts you" when they hit their kids, but "in this case it was true."

He kept telling that story to illustrate what a bad kid I was for many years. Tim once asked him why he went around telling a story about how he punched a girl, suggesting it made him seem like a jerk. My father maintained that I was an exceptionally bad kid who needed intense discipline to prevent me from becoming a criminal. He often compared me to the boy next door, Jimmy, who acted out so much that he was sent to an alternative school for bad kids. He was sure that Jimmy needed to be hit more often by his parents to be "straightened out."

Jimmy contacted me via Facebook at age 53 to inform me that she was now living as a woman. Apparently, she waited for her parents to die before transitioning. It must have been hard being a girl trapped in a boy's body in the 1970s.

Camp Massaco

Sometime in the spring of 1972, I ran into a seminary student named Walter. He had gone to elementary school with me but was studying for the priesthood, so he did not go to my high school.

Walter asked, "What are you doing this summer?"

124

I said, "Nothing." I explained that we no longer had a boat to spend long weekends on, and I never went away to camp. Family finances had gotten tight and vacations were a thing of the past.

"Well, maybe you could work with me at the YMCA Day Camp."

Getting paid to be a junior counselor was better than doing nothing, so I looked into it. There was an additional job taking attendance and maintaining order amongst the kids on the bus every morning and afternoon. Whoever did this could get an extra $60 over the summer and $35 per week. Walter and I lived near the beginning of one of these bus routes; he didn't need extra money, so I took the bus job.

This job at Camp Massaco was perfect for me. I spent eight weeks each summer for the next few years riding the bus, counting the kids and running around outside every day. I got away from home, and my job was to play with kids and make sure everyone had fun. It was like getting paid to be myself. Walter and the other counselors became my friends, and we had time to socialize like typical teenagers. Walter eventually found a girlfriend who joined the staff the next year. Corine inspired Walter to abandon the priesthood, but he continued to attend the Seminary until he graduated from high school.

At home, I was considered a problem for needing attention, talking too much, or questioning the arbitrary rules. Most high school kids I knew had some basic rules like curfews, calling home, or staying in specific areas. Every time I wanted to do anything like go to a friend's house or attend a school function, I had to ask permission. Ginny was usually able to give me a reason why I couldn't do it.

"Mom, can I go over to Nancy's house?"

"No."

"Why not?"

"You went to her house a few days ago."

"So, why can't I go today?"

"It's not necessary."

"I know it's not necessary, but I want to go."

"Stop arguing!"

Sometimes she had a rational reason, like, "I need you here to watch the phones so I can go to the store." Or, "I need you to be here for Timmy or Eileen while I go to the bank." I couldn't argue with that. Sometimes she just gave me the hairy eyeball, and I stopped pushing.

It was refreshing to work in a place where the answer was usually yes to any fun suggestion. At Camp Massaco, there were many ways to say "yes" as there were to say "no" at home. The campers played and chose what activities they wanted to do as a group. As a counselor, I was the facilitator. Any suggestion was a possibility. Rather than saying "why do you want to do that?" my job was to say, "why not?"

Later in his life, Jack would confide in Tim, "If you ever need a reason not to do something, ask your mother." I realize that part of her motivation was protective, but it seemed to have become a reflexive reaction to deny any activity, any change or any venture. Her life was hemmed in by so much responsibility that my life also had to be restricted. Preventing me from finding activities outside home gave her an in-house assistant. Ginny expected everyone in the family to deny themselves adventures and activities that might inconvenience her, put them in any kind of imagined danger, or incur any expense. I was often denied participating in activities I was willing to pay for with my own money if she considered the activity wasteful, problematic or inappropriate in any way.

During my freshman year of high school, I had a bit part in a play and worked on costumes and scenery. The Drama club rehearsed past the time the activity bus departed, so a ride home was required. I got rides from Nancy's or Linda's parents when they participated. I wanted to continue with the Drama Club in my sophomore year, but the answer was no. Jack joined in on this argument.

"Why not?" I pleaded.

"They give the lead roles to the same kids over and over, there're a bunch of snobs and weirdos," said Jack.

"We don't have time to come and get you after rehearsal," said Ginny.

"I can get a ride from Linda's parents."

"We don't want to owe them anything."

"It'd be different if you had the lead role," Jack said before I could answer Ginny.

"I don't even want the lead role; I just want a bit part and help out with scenery-"

Jack interjected, "I think the boys in the drama club are gay and I don't want you hanging around with them."

"What difference does that make?"

"I don't want you being around all those people who like acting. When we picked you up after that play you were in last year, they were all saying things like 'you were wonderful, No, YOU were wonderful!' to each other, like a bunch of fairies." Jack was homophobic; except, when it came to customers and Eileen's teacher.

So I wasn't able to continue with the Drama club. When we graduated, most of my friends from the Drama club had scholarships to elite colleges. Drama attracted some of the brainiest kids in school. I may have benefitted from spending more time with them. Danny, on the other hand, was on the wrestling team and our parents didn't complain about that inconvenience. Jack believed sports were important. We always went to the home wrestling matches and watched Danny lose every time he wrestled for four years. I was always permitted to go places to make money. If I needed a ride to babysit or work in a shop, they found a way.

My Work

Both of my parents encouraged and supported any paid employment I did. They even helped me get one job. They knew the owners of a quaint fabric and sewing shop called The Thimble who needed part-time help after school and weekends. The store sold patterns, fabric, thread, and other things known as "notions." At sixteen, I began working all day Saturdays and every Friday evening from 5-9 pm. In the summer, this job overlapped with my day camp job, but I didn't care. I was making the minimum wage, $2.01 per hour. It seemed generous. The store was relatively quiet most Friday evenings, and my job was mostly about being there in case anyone came in.

As members of the local Chamber of Commerce, my parents associated with other small business owners. I had the right kind of experience in that I had taken extra classes in home economics and knew how to sew fairly well. It was a quaint little shop in the very quaint Simsburytown Shops Shopping Center.

A pair of elderly nuns came in one evening. They had white habits and moved slowly, leaning on each other. One of them had a cane and pronounced limp. They went around touching and admiring the bolts of fabric. They talked to me a little. I had never been near a nun; both of my parents had told me horror stories about them. Once, when we visited Danny in a Catholic hospital after he had surgery, my mother had to lie to a nun who confronted us about how old Eileen and I were (There was an age limit, and I was not old enough to be there.)

The Nuns were friendly, and when they came to the counter to chat, I noticed that both had sadly misshapen faces. One had scars from what had probably been horrible acne, and the other had a crooked nose. They talked about how young nuns these days can wear pretty colors and patterns like the fabric in the shop. "We never got to wear pretty clothes" I had no idea how to respond to them. I must have nodded and smiled, thinking these are the kind of monsters I'd heard about who made little kids miserable in Catholic schools. As they were leaving they promised to pray for me. The one with the crooked nose and cane said, "Say a prayer that you never get arthritis of the knee because it is sooo painful."

I had given up praying years before, so this struck me as silly. I felt sorry for them. They had trapped themselves in a world of restrictions, and they looked like they would die in this world never even being able to enjoy the modest pleasure of choosing their clothes. I would think of them when I had my wisdom teeth removed, and the intravenous valium made me feel very depressed. The nuns' lives seemed sad, colorless, and meaningless.

If the elastic waist of the pantyhose cut into my flesh, It made me feel that my body was big and fat rather than I needed a different size. I was under the impression that my arms and legs were excessively long rather than the sleeves and pant-legs were too short. If something was too tight here or overly lose there, I believed the fault was with my body rather than the clothes.

I was under the impression that I was a failure at wearing good leather shoes because of some personal failure that made me unable to cope with the discomfort. I had no idea that my feet were unusual. The only way to be comfortable in what I would later call "lady shoes" was to get them custom made or buy high-quality shoes from a specialty store. I was uncomfortable at work because I was wearing cheap shoes and clothes that hurt.

Sometimes in the summer, the air conditioner would stop working. I was used to the heat since I worked outside all summer at my day camp job, but when the temperature went over 70 F., the preservatives began to evaporate out of the fabric, and the air became filled with formaldehyde fumes that made me sick.

I came in early each Saturday morning and vacuumed the entire store. The vacuum cleaner was old and bulky and had a very long extension cord needed to drag that monster in between all the rows of fabric. After vacuuming, I wound up the half-mile extension cord and hauled that beast back into the storage room. I often tripped over junk back there and ruined my pantyhose.

I would come out ready to start the busy Saturday crowd and the boss, Mrs. Newsom, would be scowling at me point to a spot on the floor saying, "You missed a spot." Back to the storage room I would go and drag out the beast and the extension cord again to vacuum the invisible dust off the spot. Shortly after I began my senior year in high school, Mrs. Newsom fired me. Her daughter was now old enough to work in the store, and she would be taking my place. I wasn't unhappy about it since I had decided to go to college. I could focus on getting good grades and being ready to study psychology. I still had the summer job at camp. During the school year, there was work I could sometimes get paid a few dollars for helping out with various family business activities.

Mrs. Newsom inadvertently gave me the motivation I needed to stay in school, go to college and graduate school. Every time I thought that my education was more trouble than the sacrifices required to get a degree, I thought about Mrs. Newsom pointing to the floor and saying, "You missed a spot." The idea of being stuck working for someone like her made me pay the tuition, deal with the exams, and address whatever problem I needed to overcome. She helped me see the value of an education. It was too bad there was no way to thank her for being such a sourpuss that she motivated me to make something of myself. Mrs. Newsome smoked herself to death a few years after she fired me.

For the most part, it was pleasant to work in a place where the job was to take care of beautifully printed fabric and help people find thread and buttons. There were some uncomfortable aspects. I had to wear dresses or a skirt and pantyhose. Because I was a growing teenager with body dismorphic disorder, I had no idea what size I was. Most of my dressy clothes were uncomfortable. At sixteen I was very unsure of myself. I was told when to do things differently but never thanked or encouraged for doing well.

I had friends at school who loved their part-time jobs so much they decided to go full-time when they graduated or dropped out. Living on minimum wage was possible in that time and place. If one worked 40 hours a week, one could get a used car and a cheap apartment if there was a roommate.

The idea had a certain appeal for someone like me who longed to be independent and free from overbearing parents.

At the time Jack got his real estate license, the area had several realtors who already had establishes their names and reputations in the upscale residential communities. Jack only got contracts to represent problem properties. He slowly shifted away from the role of real estate broker because nobody wanted to buy the unusual or distressed properties he listed. He might list an older home that found itself surrounded by commercial properties, e.g., gas stations that made it an undesirable place to live. He would try to sell potential buyers on the idea that if you could get the town to change the zoning, and the house could be renovated and converted to office space for doctors or lawyers to lease. He would talk about how a property could be improved, to be desirable as a rental or for resale. He ended up talking himself into buying several of these properties and making those renovations and conversions himself. Then he used those same sales pitches to convince banks to lend him money. If he couldn't sell a property, he would rent it to someone and so, he became a landlord.

As Jack made more money when he renovated, converted or developed a property, he rarely tried to sell properties for other people and instead worked on upgrading them for rent or sale. Danny and I became his on-call work crew. We hauled away junk, stuffed insulation, and did the taping and plastering of drywall. If a job required skill, like running new electrical wires, Danny was assigned to work with the electrician so he could learn the craft. I was not expected to need any building skills, so I did the unskilled work. Sometimes we got paid $5.00 for a day of work and sometimes we got nothing. As long as I lived with them as an adult, I was expected to help out with their businesses while I went to school, as well as working at other jobs.

Autism IV

Leo Kanner believed Autism was innate: that is, children were born with it; although, Hans Asperger had other ideas. So did a charlatan named Bruno Bettelheim.

Bettelheim was a charismatic man who could write beautiful prose in German and English. He was arrested in Austria in 1938 for being Jewish and sent to Dachau and then Buchenwald. He managed to get himself released and immigrated to the US in 1939. Bettelheim claimed to be a scholar who had researched and treated children with mental disorders, but whose records disappeared when he went to the concentration camps. He was able to convince the University of Chicago that he was an expert, so he was given a position there. He went on to run a school for disturbed children at the university from 1944 until 1973.

Bettelheim proceeded to promote the notion that Autism was caused by *bad* mothers who failed to hug their children properly. He claimed that these mothers sent subtle mixed messages to their babies, which in turn caused the extreme withdrawal and lack of communication seen in children brought to his clinic. Like Sigmund Freud, this theory traced most cases of emotional disturbance to early childhood experience. Bettelheim blamed mothers for destroying the psyches of their children. He is responsible for the popularity of the term "refrigerator mother," (Bettelheim, Bruno. *The Empty Fortress: Infantile Autism and the Birth of the Self.* New York: Simon & Schuster, 1967.), which described a cold woman who damages children by starving them of love.

Bettelheim claimed to be able to cure Autistic children by providing the right kind of love. This concept, which has since been debunked, became very popular in the United States and set back research into the proper understanding and treatment of Autistic children for decades. Back in 1960 when Eileen first showed signs of withdrawal and uncommunicativeness, the void in public understanding was unfortunately filled by Bettelheim. He had the easy answer to the difficult question of, "what happened to my child?"

Autism, he maintained, is caused by cold mothers. It is cured by "love." People, for want of better answers, believed him. Bettelheim would later be found out as a fraud, a cruel egomaniac who by misrepresenting his credentials was able to garner prestige and funding from the University, and control over the school where he acted as a tyrant to clients and staff (Ronald Angres, "Who, Really was Bruno Bettelheim? When a famous man dies and is eulogized, those who knew him often feel a shock of recognition." *Commentary Magazine* [October 01, 1997]). He had a mysterious air of authority and wisdom honed in the concentration camps. He made the most of the sympathy and respect that his holocaust survivor status gave him (M. Finn, "In the case of Bruno Bettelheim." *First Things* (74) 44–8, [1997]).

Eileen was unlucky enough to develop Autism. Our parents, along with the parents of most Autistic children in mid-twentieth century America, were doubly unlucky to have the disorder appear when a proper diagnosis did not exist in the either the medical or mainstream literature. If parents sought help, they got blamed for destroying their child's mental health.

IN THE SWING

Swinging! Swinging!

I like to swing in the softness

— — And then my feet touch the ground

— And I make a big hole.

-Eileen

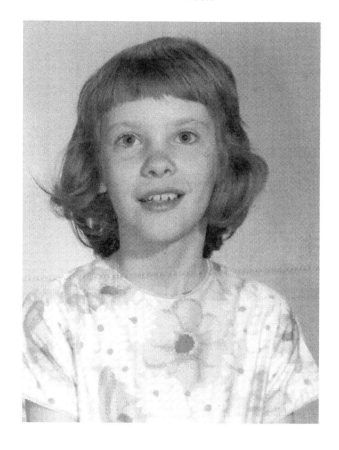

Chapter 6
  Baking Cookies

"That's Different."

In high school, I was finding acceptance and my voice as well as sympathy from other misunderstood kids and empathic teachers. Outside my home, I was developing a personality that was fun and goofy.

I had given up trying to be pretty, not believing I had the basics of beauty. My mother's looks set a standard far beyond my potential, so I attempted to develop in other ways. Being witty and mouthy was perhaps a characteristic and temperament I learned and inherited from my father. It came naturally to me, and my friends seem to appreciate it most of the time. When I was sixteen, my mother tried to curb this part of my personality. She took me aside to inform me humor was not something that women could do, so I should stop trying. I asked her about the famous female comedians of the era (The word back then was comediennes). "What about Totie Fields and Joan Rivers?" She said, with a completely straight face, "That's different, they're Jewish."

This was the funniest thing I ever heard her say, and I burst out laughing. She said something hilarious to convince me that women weren't funny. She had also made an ethnic slur, which was odd in itself, since being from immigrant stock, and being in the employment business, my parents were typically very vocal regarding ethnic equality. My mother got furious with me for laughing so hard. She demanded to know what was so funny. I repeated her words, "That's different, they're Jewish."

She insisted she never said that, seconds after having spoken. When I related the story to the rest of the family, she refused to admit that was what she said. This was one of the many times when she would say, "Never write about your life, Sharon, or if you do, leave me out of it!" Whenever this story came up again (and it did come up, since it was a great story), she kept repeating that she never said it. I persisted in recalling it, and wondered why she should not want credit for spontaneously throwing out such a great line.

Decades later, when the story came up yet again, and she felt the need to clarify her original meaning, she finally admitted that she had indeed said something that sounded like an excellent joke. She tried to explain that Jewish people had a culture of self-deprecating humor, so it was acceptable for them, but Sharon was not Jewish, so being funny was not appropriate or possible for her. It seems that 40 years later the idea that women can't be funny is still being debated.

Baking Cookies

Baking was a chore assigned to Eileen and me. At first, I was enthusiastic about this responsibility. I was trusted to read the recipe or the directions if it was a box mix. I preheated the oven and made sure to set the timer after it went in the oven. Eileen would mix and help as I directed her. I would clean up. Then I became a teenager, and there were things I preferred to spend my time doing rather than baking. I wanted to be as skinny as the skinniest girls I knew. I started teaching Eileen to do most of it herself. She was able to follow the directions on the boxes and eventually she needed minimal help with baking. Ginny would not permit her to turn on the oven, or let me teach her how. When

Eileen wanted to bake, she had to ask me to preheat the oven. Then she would follow the directions up to putting the pans in the oven. Eileen then had to seek me out and ask me to set the timer. She did the rest, including cleaning up.

Our family ate dessert after both lunch and dinner. I'm not sure why this was the custom. Maybe it was to indulge the desire for sweets both of my parents had. It may have been a way to get cheap calories into the skinny kids. When the budget was tight, we saved the family money making desserts instead of buying extra calories in readymade desserts.

One day, when Timmy was nine years old, he wanted to do some baking and asked for my help. We made brownies, and when it was time to clean up, he refused to help, saying something about boys not washing dishes. It was the norm in our house that Ginny, Eileen or I always washed the dishes. Timmy's belief that his status as a boy automatically meant that he could skip out on kitchen clean-up was understandable, but wrong as far as I was concerned. I became the evil big sister and demanded that he help wash the bowls and utensils. After all, the baking project was his idea. I was not going to have him order me to clean up after his cooking project simply because he was a boy. I think I made him cry and had to use my superior size and strength to insist he do some of the washing. Timmy made the mistake of expecting me to conform to the gender norms set by our parents. He had a rude awakening that day.

I was in an odd situation. Jack and my brothers took out the trash each week and made repairs around the house. They also took care of cars. I had all the typically female responsibilities like answering the phones, kitchen work, and looking after my siblings. I was also expected to shovel snow, help with building projects and do yard work.

I noticed that Ginny's work was continuous while men's work was occasional. The traditional division of labor made no sense when Ginny had more duties at home but just as much or more responsibility for the business. She expected respect for her business skill and knowledge, but she never requested my father's or brothers' help with any of her domestic responsibilities. She often made it difficult for Jack to help. Ginny ridiculed his attempts to assist in the kitchen and failure to learn to shop.

Ginny was protective of her domain and worked herself to exhaustion keeping most others away. She had me trained to do a few things and trusted me to take care of menial tasks like loading and unloading the dishwasher, or assisting with no more than one part of meal preparation, but if I wanted to take care of cooking dinner by myself, the answer was no. There were so many ways that Ginny and I failed to understand each other.

Ginny was never even remotely a feminist. She held fast to tradition and believed in conservative traditions and values. Yet she had no love for organized religion and never attended church after the local priest Father Shae, had a problem with our baby brother's middle name not being saintly enough. He suggested changing it from Darin to Darius for the formal christening. That may have been strike three for the Catholic Church as far as my mother was concerned. There would be no formal christening for Timmy.

Ginny only attended church for funerals after that. She liked the name she chose for him. She once told me she planned to name me Timothy if I had been born a boy. I think she loved my name as well.

Jack insisted we all have Irish names. Of course, he wanted to name his firstborn son after the father he could not remember. She was able to convince my father that Sharon was an Irish name, which it is not. She lorded her better grades and more detailed knowledge skills over him that way and insisted that she was right. It became apparent to Jack and the rest of us that it was useless to argue. I seem to have had a harder time learning that lesson than the others in the family.

Why wouldn't Ginny want to have equal rights as a woman, and for other women to have the same rights and privileges as men? She was smart, capable, and ambitious. But she preferred the notion that she deserved special protection and privilege as a woman. She told me as much. In the days when to be sexually active meant risking motherhood, and motherhood required a certain amount of dependency, a protected status might have made sense. As an unusually beautiful woman, she was accustomed to deference. She preferred holding the position of the hidden power behind the man that many women with intelligence and attractiveness can assume.

Being in control while not appearing to have authority has the advantage of being able to blame failure on the puppet-leader while taking half the credit for every success. Half is better than none to a person who grew up poor. She was unable to appreciate that not all women would want, or be able, to get themselves into this kind of arrangement.

Cars

I had difficulty learning to drive. In addition to being the kind of distracted daydreamer who has problems maintaining focus while multi-tasking, I had very inconsistent training. I took driver education in school at the end of my junior year when I turned seventeen. It came at no extra cost with the rest of our free education (bought for by the high property taxes and fear of Communism). I attended the classes after school and we watched movies about kids joy-riding after the prom and getting killed. I memorized the booklet, took the test, and got my learner's permit.

Learning the rules was not hard, but learning to drive was a whole other issue. The driver-education class entitled me to six hours of on-the-road lessons. I took the course in the spring of 1974, spending my first ninety-minute road lesson accompanied by a big homely science teacher with an off-beat sense of humor. As a passenger, I had often watched the yellow or white lines from the car window, often entering a state of mesmerized oblivion as a result. Staying in the lane by watching the painted line disappear under the left front fender made sense to me.

"Your driving is erratic," the teacher said.

"I'm following the line in the middle of the road."

"You're doing WHAT?" he said.

"I'm trying to keep the car lined up with the line," I explained.

"Where are you looking?" he asked.

"At the front corner of the car and the line in the middle of the road; isn't that what the line is for?"

"NO! Don't look there. You should be looking..." he pointed emphatically toward the middle of the windshield, "... out there!"

Having a trained driving instructor helped me solve that problem. But I had other misconceptions and habits that would cause me to fail the road test more than once. My next ninety-minute lesson was over a month later, and although this time I was able to point my eyes in the right direction, I still needed to learn how to do all the other driving tasks that I had forgotten about in the intervening weeks. In driver-education class, they insisted that you needed much more than six hours of practice to be a proficient driver. I had difficulty getting my parents to let me practice driving.

My parents had no patience for teaching me. The few times they let me drive with them in the car, they began yelling at the least little error, real or imagined. This made me so nervous I couldn't focus and ended up making more mistakes. Within five minutes they would say, "Pull over and let me drive." Once, I asked Dad if I could practice driving and the answer, as usual, was no. In exasperation, I asked, "How the hell am I ever gonna get my license if you won't let me practice?" He said, "Don't you 'how the hell' me, or I'll break your ass!"

Over the summer I forgot how to drive. I had to wait until the fall to get another ninety-minute driving lesson from the big homely science teacher. I had another one about two months later. Each lesson was like starting over. Lesson time was wasted as I tried to calm down and accept criticism, after having both my parents scream at me every other time I was behind the wheel. I failed the road test at the Department of Motor Vehicles (DMV), and my learner's permit expired.

My parents decided that they couldn't afford the cost of adding another driver to the insurance plan. My big brother was driving by now and could drop me off or pick me up from my part-time job. I was not permitted to be in any school activities. There was bus I could ride to school, and another bus that could take me to my summer camp job. So that's the way it was; I was nineteen when I finally got a driver's license.

After he completed high school, Dan started attending a technical college. He bought an old pickup truck, and this enabled him to commute to school and do some heavy work for Jack. The truck had a plow attachment, and when it snowed, Dan and I would take care of the rental properties. Dan drove and cleared the snow with the plow, and I did the shoveling of walkways and other places the plow couldn't go. We might earn us $5 or $10 each if there was any money to pay us.

Moving large amounts of snow with a shovel gave me a sense of satisfaction. It was nice when Jack trusted me to work independently. When I worked for Ginny, she hovered and dictated so many details that I felt stupid, lazy, and useless. I enjoyed shoveling snow, at home and the rental properties; nobody told me how to do it.

I loved working at summer camp. It hardly seemed like work at all. It was nice to be free of thinking about what I looked like—there were no mirrors at camp. I wore old, ratty clothes which was normal. My hair was a mess from going in and out of the water with the kids, and that too was normal. My skin was not perfect, but it was tanned. I had no hair products to make me look like someone else, and not much in the way of clothes to cover the imperfections of my body.

The lessons imposed on me by my upper-class schoolmates and Ginny proved to be lies. A girl with cheap, ill-fitting clothes, acne, and no makeup, and no time to hide her physical or social flaws could be useful, liked and admired—perhaps even desired. I could be myself, and everything was OK. I was being paid to be myself and I could be creative, social, spontaneous and casual, and it was all accepted and appreciated.

Of course at Camp Massaco we were all young and healthy people dressed minimally in the summer heat, and with the hormones of adolescence we responded to the pheromones we released into the air around us. By contrast, my parents' obsession with making my hair look acceptable and my clothes decent seemed wrong, judgmental, and outdated to me. The standards of the upper-middle class kids at my high school regarding fashion and coolness began to strike me as foolish and made me feel sorry for them. I looked down at their values and felt that mine were better.

As my teen years passed the family finances became more strained. I dressed more and more like a hippie and less and less like the respectable young republican my parents wished me to be. Ginny would have preferred I wear preppy clothes to school, but there was no budget for that, so I was free to wear my faded jeans and embroidered creations. As I progressed through high school, the jerks outgrew the need to belittle those who were a bit different. Some of the kids from the wealthier side of town turned out to be very friendly and eager to get to know me.

A somewhat dim girl from the more affluent side of town once was talking to me about shopping, where the best clothes could be bought and which records she planned to get. I told her that I couldn't buy clothes and music for fun. "You work, right?" she asked. "Yes, I have a job at a store, and I'm a camp counselor during the summer." She asked me, "If you don't buy clothes and records with your money, what do you use it for?" "I'm saving it to pay for college."

This confused her. "Your parents have a business, don't they?" "Yes." "Why don't they pay for your college?" I don't remember how I answered that, but I remember feeling sorry for her being so ignorant about the lives of other people. I was developing a reverse snobbery in response to elite Simsbury High School kids. Tariffville was really only a small step down economically from most of Simsbury, but we had a fierce pride about our village. We called it T-Ville and proudly wore this identity in yearbooks and social circles, like Hester Prynne's Scarlet Letter. The slightly better off people from Simsbury couldn't understand this pride.

The same girl who could not fathom parents not being able to pay for college once said, "You're from Tariffville? You don't seem it." I tried not to burst out laughing at her. She was trying to be nice, but she just didn't understand.

Perhaps because Timmy was so sick and near death as a baby and toddler, he grew into a happy and easily amused little boy. He liked hanging around with his older siblings. He knew how to avoid being a pest and appreciated any attention he received. He was happy to watch and listen as Dan, and I played checkers, talked, or drank beer. The drinking age was 18 back then. When Dan had a job, he purchased Heineken beer to drink and share.

Timmy found a cereal box with a chess set printed on it and asked me to help him learn to play it. We cut out the cardboard chessmen. They were designed as two tiny pieces of cardboard fitted together so that they would stand up on the printed chess board. I read the directions, and we began to play chess. Soon Dan wanted to play, and we took turns playing with Timmy. We like it so well that we purchased a set with plastic pieces. In the evenings Dan and I would play chess by ourselves. Dan drank beer after beer. Dan was better at chess than I was, but as he drank, I won more games.

Dan's pick-up truck was old, and the engine blew while Dan drove home from school. Black smoke filled the streets as the truck limped home. Dan rebuilt the engine in the garage and life went on. Jack often asked Dan and me to take the trash to the dumps in Dan's pick-up truck. Timmy would jump up and down with joy at the idea of coming along. At the dump, we tended to poke around for good stuff or interesting things that other people threw away.

This wasn't just recreation. We occasionally cleaned out the garage and had a yard sale with all the stuff we had collected, and any household items we no longer had any use for. There were times that Ginny took the proceeds from a yard sale straight to the grocery store to buy food. We kids could keep the money that we made selling our own items. Timmy was able to make some cash for himself by refinishing furniture that other people threw away and then selling it at our yard sale.

Dan had a full beard from high school and we were both tall. When we were out and about running errands for our parents, we were often mistaken for a married couple. Or if Timmy was with us, they saw a family with a little boy.

One sunny spring day, Ginny threw out a box of canceled checks that were nearly a decade old. The checks had their legal names on them. Dan, Timmy and I took the trash to the dumps as usual. We had some fun tossing the checks in the air and watching them flutter around. I picked up a check and kidded Timmy about the diaper service charges from when he was a baby. Another customer at the dump enjoyed watching us. He must have read the names on the checks, because as he drove away, he shouted, "Bye John! Bye Virginia!"

Sex, Drugs, and Rock & Roll

Because Simsbury was a sprawling suburban town filled with families that from the baby boom, the buses that ferried us to middle and high school made two runs each morning and afternoon. If you lived far from school (I lived five miles away) you were picked up and dropped off at school first, then waited in the homeroom while the buses went back and collected kids who lived closer to school. Those who lived less than one mile were expected to walk or ride bikes. Students with indulgent parents got driven, and then provided with a car when they were old enough to drive.

From sixth through twelfth grade, I got on the bus at 7:00, arrived about twenty minutes later and waited until 8:00, when they took attendance, made announcements, we pledged allegiance to the flag, and then went to class.

The advantage of the first morning bus was that you could walk out of school, hop on at 2:30 and be home by 3:00. All through middle school and ninth grade, Nancy got on the bus at the first morning stop and saved the seat next to her for me. We talked all the way to and from school and often visited each other's homes.

While I had never been encouraged or inclined to do extracurricular activities, Nancy was bold and adventurous. Nancy had the desire to try out for things and participate in after-school activities.

Kids who arrived by bus and stayed for after-school activities could take one of the activity busses home. They left at 4:00 and each went to different parts of town. I took the late bus a few times during my freshman year when I was best friends with Nancy. The activity bus covered more area than the regular busses so it took an hour to get to my stop.

On those long rambling late bus rides to Tariffville, Nancy initiated conversations with the bus driver and got to know him by name. He was a large grandfatherly black man named Ross. Nancy told me he was a minister and good to talk to. After Nancy went off to live with her mother, I would chat with Ross and sometimes talk him into driving me all the way into our housing development, saving me the half-mile walk.

Once, on a warm spring day, when I was the only one who showed up for the activity bus, Ross made an interesting suggestion. "Say, since you are the only one on the bus and the depot is close to school and your house is on my way home, how about we go drop off this bus, and I'll take you home in my old rattletrap car?"

It seemed the only kind thing to do; he was a tired old man who probably started work at 6:00 in the morning. So I said, "Sure." He either suggested I keep quiet about it, or I sensed he was breaking a rule. He drove me home and thanked me for letting him use his car. It was a rare situation where I could do a favor for an adult that was appreciated. It seemed like no big deal and I never told anyone about it.

Sometime during the following school year, another bus driver had taken Ross's place; an older, chatty man. I asked him what happened to Ross. He said, "Oh, they don't let Ross drive the bus anymore. It seems he was too friendly with some girls."

I was shocked and worried about Ross. The new guy said, "Oh he's Ok, they have him driving delivery trucks now." I was sorry that Ross would not have the company of kids while he drove, and worried that he might be lonely. I wondered if some bigoted parents didn't like the idea of a black man speaking to their daughter. I spent time alone with him and never sensed anything creepy about him.

It was an unseasonably warm day in late February when I was permitted to exit school about five minutes early because I was carrying a cumbersome art project. I had burlap stretched over a large frame and bags of old socks and nylon hose. I was going to make a hooked rug on burlap depicting Adam and Eve in the Garden of Eden. Adam was going to be blond and white and Eve was going to be black and beautiful. I had started the project in school and planned to complete it at home. To prevent it getting crushed in the rush for busses lined up and ready to take us to our respective neighborhoods, the teacher monitoring the crowd let me slip out early. I tapped on the bus door, and a new bus driver let me in.

He asked about my project. So I sat in the seat closest to the front of the bus and told him about it. He asked which art teacher I had and then revealed he had the same art teacher a few years earlier and had enjoyed her class. He was now working on becoming a professional photographer. He asked me to tell Mrs. Dicosimo that Ricky Rooney said hello.

One or two afternoons later I hopped on the bus. Ricky commented on the chilly rain and fog. I said, "I think the moisture in the air increases your psychic power." He was intrigued. I was sixteen going on seventeen; He was twenty-one going on fourteen. So there I was, at the age of consent in Connecticut, getting all this attention from a good-looking man with dark hair, a goatee and a mustache.

We talked about art and our mutual hiking territories around Tariffville. He had grown up nearby and graduated just before I started high school. He had been in the Navy. He had a bad attitude about his time in the service because the recruiter promised he could go to photography school, but he wound up having to learn to operate radio communication systems instead. The military was downsizing because the Vietnam War was winding down and all the Americans were leaving. A few Air Force facilities managed the Cold War with intercontinental ballistic missiles aimed at the USSR, so the Army, Navy, and Marine Corps offered early honorable discharges to all the surplus personnel who wanted out.

I sat near the front of the bus for the rest of the week chatting with Ricky. Near the end of the week, he invited me to meet him that weekend at the trail to Laurel Hill. I often took long walks in the woods or by the river by myself when the weather was amenable. I told Ginny where I was going and went for a long hike with Ricky. When it was time for us to go separate directions to where we lived, he kissed me. I kissed him back.

After that, catching the bus at 7:00 was easier than it had been before. Ricky and I talked and looked at each other via the large rear-view mirror at the front of the bus. I could only see the top half of his face, and watched his thick black expressive eyebrows rise and fall when he spoke. He had my phone number and soon called me for a real date: dinner and a movie.

One would think my parents would disapprove. They did, but had decided between themselves that the best tactic was to say nothing about this relationship because they believed that forbidding it would cause me to run away with him. I wasn't interested in running away. I just wanted to lose my virginity. I accomplished this goal a few days before my seventeenth birthday.

Once, in the short time I dated Ricky, I had a nightmare in which I married him and ended up living in a crappy apartment, taking in ironing and laundry from better off people. When I woke up, I was more certain than ever that I wanted to go to college and have fun before I settled down. I had already decided I would be closer to age thirty than twenty when I married. I wanted to have lots of lovers and adventures before settling down with a husband and family.

When summer began, I had my camp job as well as the Friday evening and all-day Saturday job at The Thimble. Ricky was more interested in getting high and having adventures than making something of his life. He talked about wanting to be a professional photographer. He had a few of his photos enlarged, framed, and on display in one local restaurant, but he was only working part-time and seemed to be stuck living with his parents indefinitely. He spent more time playing than working toward his goals. I was going to school, working two jobs and planning my future. I was too busy to spend much time with him. The amount of time and effort Ricky spent on getting and using drugs seemed like a waste of time and money to me.

I was too busy to spend much time or energy on him. My summer camp colleagues were compelling company. I was beginning to find Ricky kind of clueless by comparison. I decided to break up with him. One midsummer Sunday afternoon Ricky visited and we hung out in the upstairs sitting room. I rambled on about our relationship not going anywhere. He sat, slumped over and looking sad. I thought that I had finally gotten my point across. Then he said, "You know what I think the problem is?" "What?" "I think you're falling in love with me." I don't recall what I said after that, but it was over. Eileen always had an odd reaction to my relationship with Ricky.

Danny, Eileen and I were now living in the upstairs addition Jack had finally finished. We each had our own room. There was a sitting room at the top of the stairs, connecting to our bedrooms. Eileen drifted silently through this room while Randy and I sat together talking or sometimes kissing. She may have been confused to see her younger sister behaving as a teenager. Maybe she was surprised by the fact that I was engaging in adult behavior with a man. That my childhood was ending.

After I broke up with Ricky, Eileen asked me, "Is Mr. Rooney going to be visiting again?" Perhaps with the "mister" she was commenting on him being too old for me. Eileen would stay in a childlike dependent state indefinitely while I grew up. I was leaving her behind in fairy land and entering the world of adults.

Carol's Mom Comes to the Rescue

My parents helped to sell a piece of property that contained the inventory of a music store that had closed in the early 1960s. The buyers wanted an empty property, so rather than wholesaling the music store inventory, Ginny and Jack moved it all into a vacant rental space they had in The Building. Simsbury didn't have a music store, and they figured they could fill that niche and make some money if they opened one.

The inventory included some valuable vintage electric guitars and a few violins. It also had about sixty accordions, beautifully decorated with inlaid wood and mother-of-pearl designs, but nobody wanted them. The mid-to-late 1970s was not a good time for accordion music.

By my senior year in high school, my grades and SAT score were good enough for me to be considered college material. I had decided to major in psychology with the plan to attend graduate school to become a psychologist; or, perhaps a social worker or counselor. Because I had very little money, and my grades had only recently improved, I would have to start at a community college.

I still could not drive, and buses did not run as far as the suburb where we lived. I had to commute to Greater Hartford Community College. It was near Hartford State Technical College where Dan was working on his associate's degree (Those two schools would later merge into one). He could drop me off and pick me up on his way to and from school.

I loved going to school there and began to do very well. It was a bit of a culture shock to go from a ritzy suburban high school with high academic standards to an urban community college filled with city folks and older students returning to school after being knocked around by life for a few years. As a white kid and a recent high school graduate, I was a minority.

While attending community college, I was still living with my parents and was expected to help out with cleaning, taking care of my siblings and working in the music store.

I became a valuable resource because I knew how to play guitar, could tune all the stringed instruments, and advise them on what popular music and guitar accessories to stock. I also would be asked to mind the music store while I studied so they wouldn't have to pay a clerk. It was usually quiet there, and I could get a lot of schoolwork done in between customers.

If there were coins in the cash drawer, Ginny asked me to set aside all the quarters and dimes dated before 1964 because the silver content was worth more than face value. Jack was still accusing me of being the enemy in the culture war he believed was destroying the country, but when I cut my hair shorter and became more valuable to his business ventures, he attacked me less often. Ginny was treating me with more respect as well. I was learning to keep my opinions more to myself and was stepping on fewer emotional landmines.

My best friend from high school moved to Boston. Carol became my new best friend. She lived a short distance away. We had known each other since kindergarten. She shared her kittens with me. Carol had stopped attending school regularly when her parents went through an ugly divorce. She had worse times in school and at home than I had, and when she dropped out we began hanging out. Carol later earned her GED and took a few college classes.

The long hard winter of 1975 broke, and I was looking for adventure on one beautiful March day. I had noticed a culvert I wanted to explore that went under the highway to Hartford, about two miles outside of Tariffville. Carol and I hiked to the culvert and walked through it, hunched over. It was about four feet in diameter and sloped gently downward, so the beginning of this trek wasn't too daunting. The highway was about ninety feet across, and our muscles were getting sore by the time we saw daylight near the end.

Then we noticed the water.

The culvert tube was submerged. The air temperature was warm for March in northern Connecticut, about 55 degrees. The water had only recently thawed from ice. At this point, we had to make a decision. We could wade through two-foot deep water six-feet across. Or, we could turn around and force our cramping leg muscles through a return trip up an incline rather than a down as before. We decided on going forward; and through the water, soaking our shoes, socks, and jeans. Having reached the far end, we needed to walk back home.

After hiking two miles in the brisk spring air with sore muscles, in wet clothes, we reached the village. We still had another mile to get to where we lived, and no desire to continue. There was a phone booth in front of the little grocery store. Carol called her mom, and soon she arrived in her battered car and drove us to their house. During the ride, Carol told her about our adventure. Her mom expressed nothing but concern and sympathy.

I knew that had I called my parents I might have been given a ride, but undoubtedly would have been in for a lecture about my stupidity. I would have been punished by being grounded indefinitely (yes, I could still be grounded at age nineteen), and ridiculed for years afterward. I was so grateful to be able to go to Carol's house and wait for my clothes to dry before going home.

I thought Carol's mom was a rare and unusual kind of mother. She was special to her daughter, and that made her the type of mom that people need. It would be a long time before I realized that this kind of mother was not rare. The mother I had was the exception.

Ginny once told me that if I ever found myself in a situation where I was in a car with a drunk driver, that I should call and she would give me a ride, no matter where I was. I remember thinking that I would rather risk death in a car accident than recrimination for getting myself into a dangerous situation in the first place. I was afraid to ask my parents for any kind of help. I would keep hidden from my parents all the problems that were possible to hide, avoiding their verbal attacks and constant belittling about my previous failings.

Soon Carol met Ben, and the two got married. I was honored to be her "best woman." We had a bridal shower at my house. Ginny had a recipe for sangria, which was somewhat high in alcohol. The party was sweet, with older ladies and us younger women. After all the older women left, Ginny and Jack went to bed. Ben, his friends, and my brother Dan joined us in finishing the sangria. Ben took Carol home and I can't remember how the rest of us ended up naked in the swimming pool.

Working My Way through College

As I transitioned from high school to college, Camp Massaco changed management and brought in a new staff. I was at loose ends for the first few weeks of summer 1975 until I found a new job at a residential camp for New Yorkers. Lenox Hill Neighborhood Association ran a facility in Litchfield, Connecticut. Half of the counselors came from the city and half came from other places scattered around Litchfield.

Ginny had a meltdown when I told her I wanted to work at a residential camp. But I needed a job, and Jack probably wanted me out of the house. So Ginny lost her helper for the summer. Jack lost the thorn in his side, the wedge between his wife and him, and I got to live in the woods with city kids.

My co-counselor Ann Marie was happy to have my help. She asked me in her thick Brooklyn accent, "Are you out dawzey? Can you make a fiyah?" Yes, I was, and yes I could. I had perfected the one-match fire at Camp Massacco when we had weekly over-nights for the older kids.

I lived in the woods all summer, working with inner-city kids from 7:00 in the morning until 9:00 in the evening, six days a week. Being away from my parents was wonderful. I also enjoyed being around the staff that were mostly college students who enjoyed working with kids and being outdoors.

The city kids were more interesting than the suburban day camp kids I had worked with. The New York kids were a mixture of rich, poor, Black, White, and Puerto Rican. They were more outspoken and independent than suburban kids. The groups quickly became tribes that we counselors could barely control. Taking a hike involved following them, listening to them sing songs and shout chants that were often off-color or inappropriate for kids:

Yo Ma! Yo Pa!
Your greasy granny gotta hole in her panties
She gotta big behind like Frankenstein

She go beep beep beep down Sesame Street
Abba Dabba soda Cracker
Beat the back of my butt!
OOH!
Beat the back of my butt!

I surmised that the city kids were more independent because they could use public transportation rather than waiting to be chauffeured by their parents. It could be that the city culture and suburban cultures attracted different types of families. I found the city kids more interesting. On the first day of one session at Lenox hill Camp, I had an interesting exchange with a ten year-old boy.

"Man! I hate Connecticut—there's too god-damned many misquitas heah. I'm going back to da city." "How are you going to get back to the city," I asked him? He looked at me like I was crazy and said, "I'll take a bus!" I told him, "There are no buses out here in the woods." He gave me that look again and said, "Well, den, I'll take a cab!"

The job at Lenox Hill Camp paid me room and board and $500. It cost $100 for each semester at Greater Hartford Community College to take five classes. I was allowed to take more classes for the same price after proving I could handle more. Books and other supplies cost another $100. Since I lived rent-free with parents, my $500 could buy more than a year of college, including coffee and lunch at the cafeteria.

The next summer at Lenox Hill Camp led up to my second year at college. Dan graduated in 1976 with his engineering associate's degree and would not be able to drop me off on his way to his college. He now had a full-time job. I was nineteen and would need to be able to drive to continue going to college. So I hired a professional driving instructor to help me get ready to take the road test.

He was a creepy old man who liked to stroke my thigh and made suggestive remarks about "parking." I threatened to drive off the road if he kept touching me and he complied. I kept paying him for lessons until I was able to parallel park and drive well enough to pass the road test. I needed three hours of instruction to learn the techniques I needed and used some of my yoga breathing and meditation to deal with his groping and my nervousness. I had become a more disciplined person. To complete my second year of college I was allowed to drive to school in either the rusting 1966 Thunderbird or the fake wood-paneled station wagon.

Exploration

The 1970s was a time for seeking an alternative education unfettered by the unsettled turmoil of the 1960s. The Hare Krishnas danced and begged in public places in bright saffron-colored robes with their heads shaved except for a skinny ponytail at the back of their heads. They were militant vegetarians. Rich kids would go to India to study Hindu spirituality in Ashrams. There were cults, sects, and organizations of all sorts. Each was promising a better way to be happy, free, enlightened, or saved. The Children of God was a communal Christian group that practiced free love and begged for money in the streets. They took in lost and homeless youth and transformed them into beggars and prostitutes to support a life of prayer and *love*.

Early in my study of psychology, I was captivated by the notion of how readily people can surrender themselves to charismatic leaders. The stories about the Manson family, Patty Hearst, and my study of cults made me wary and skeptical about all kinds of leaders and groups. I learned about Scientology and how they recruited people with promises of super-powers if you studied with them long enough.

One of my first college term papers was on brainwashing and how it was being done in the US today. Among my references was a book by George Malko on Scientology, which had to be removed from all libraries and bookstores because of lawsuits filed by the Church of Scientology. I was becoming an adult, beginning to revel in freedom from of my oppressive parents, going to college, and finding out how to use my brain and make use of all the knowledge available in libraries and schools. I was deeply disturbed that some people chose to relinquish all their freedom and turn their thoughts and decisions over to a leader. It seemed so easy for a religious leader or other charlatan to take advantage of the human need for community. I learned to question authority and think critically before accepting new ideas.

The more I studied about people, who joined cults and extreme political groups, the more I found that those followers were a lot like me: searching, confused, and frightened. I felt lucky to have discovered the methods used by cult leaders and other charismatic charlatans before becoming the prey of some nefarious leader. My family situation of not being wanted, accepted, trusted or liked made me the sort of person who was vulnerable to recruitment by a cult. My stubborn, independent streak may have been something prevented that from happening, but after learning about others who fell into these groups, I began to think that very few people are immune.

There are many techniques used to gain control over others. They include isolation, stress, simplistic ideology and 'love bombing'. Love bombing is a technique where a new member is surrounded by emotional support and friendship as long as they behave appropriately and followed like good sheep.

When I was twenty-one, the Reverend Jim Jones was the leader of a Christian cult that induced over 900 people to follow him to Guyana. The year I started graduate school he forced them all to drink poison when the heroic (and closeted gay) Congressman Leo Ryan investigated. The term "drink the Kool-Aid" came from this incident. Pictures of the bloated bodies of men, women, and many children horrified everyone who saw them reported across the media. Congressman Ryan was machine-gunned to death trying to rescue a few members who wanted to leave, just before the epic mass murder/suicide.

Financial Aid

My college career was more like a sprint than a marathon. I raced ahead as soon as I started by taking something called CLEP (College Level Examination Program) exams. For $20 I could take a test that covered the contents of one college class. If I scored better than 50% of the scores of actual students, the college would give full credit. Thanks to my extensive reading and excellent science teachers, I got credit for almost a year's worth of college in this fashion. Then after getting good grades, they let me take six classes a semester for the low, low price of $100.

Dr. Hershberger taught Psychology 101, the introductory course. He was a large old red-faced man, a proponent of the Behavioral technique (incentives, rewards, punishments), and ran his class according to behavioral theory. He would sit on the desk in front of the room, and start each class by saying, "I am going to cover chapter seven today. If you have not taken all the quizzes up to this unit, you must stay for the lecture. The rest of you may split." The tests and quizzes were given in a lab rather than in class, and students could work ahead. I blew through the 16-week course in just a few weeks, and after I aced Psychology 101, I was offered a part-time job in the psychology lab.

Dr. Hershberger's class covered ten units of a textbook. There were three "forms" of quizzes for each unit, consisting of multiple choice questions. He would deliver a lecture for each chapter. After students had listened to the lectures, or studied the unit and felt ready for the quiz, they could take the quiz in the psychology lab. As the student assistant in the psychology lab, I would administer Form A the first time a student took a quiz, and go over their mistakes with them if they didn't pass. They could take Form B after learning from their mistakes, and take Form C as an alternative if they didn't pass Form B. If they didn't pass any of the quizzes they had to take the highest failing grade out of three and then proceed to the next unit.

I used my wages to buy books, coffee, and the occasional pizza or drinks with classmates at local bars. The drinking age had been lowered to eighteen, so this was legal at the time. I was happily putting myself through college. I managed to earn nearly three years worth of credit in two years. I was motivated and interested in learning like never before and getting mostly A's with the occasional B.

When Dan and I began to bring home dean's list report cards after having been under-achievers at Simsbury High School, our parents said that college must have gotten easier since they had attended. Dan and I occasionally got back-handed compliments but were rarely told that we were doing well. They didn't celebrate our accomplishments the way that the families in books and television did. We continued to argue. During some of those arguments, they suggested I needed to take a course in Logic. I got an A in Logic and still couldn't communicate with them.

I was able to pay for my community college tuition and books with my own money, but life would have been more comfortable had I been able to get the grants that I was eligible for. I might have chosen to go away to college or live in an apartment near school rather than with my parents. I would not have had to get a loan to pay for my third and final undergraduate year.

But Ginny refused to sign any applications I brought back from the financial aid office. I was perplexed when she, who made all the financial decisions, refused to sign. Was she afraid of some kind of tax audit? The family businesses were not making money, and I was rarely paid more than a few dollars for the many hours labor I provided them. Did she think I was not deserving of government "charity," like that time she wouldn't let the priest buy me a dress that fit?

My availability to work at home may have been the reason. Maybe it was just the thing that Ginny needed to make her life workable as the partner, administrator, and bookkeeper of the family businesses. When I was gone, she was tied to the home office with no one to cover for her if she went out for groceries or anything else. Maybe this was the real reason I was not allowed to get a driver's license, not that the auto insurance would go too high, as they claimed.

I asked Ginny to stop declaring me as a dependent. The businesses were doing so poorly by now they weren't paying income tax anyway, so she agreed. After three years of not being declared a dependent, I could apply for financial aid independently. What I did not realize was, in my rush to complete college, I had finished my bachelor's degree, and Pell and equal opportunity grants could only be applied to undergraduate work. I had inadvertently worked my way past being eligible.

Me, My Sister and Deacon Walters

Tariffville is a tiny town where people know too much about everyone else's business. Most of the school staff lived in the neighborhood.

As I wrote earlier, in 1966 the child of the principal and administrator who kicked my sister out of school would follow me home saying, "Your sister's retarded, your brother's retarded, your' whole family is retarded. You even have a retarded dog." That was Elaine Walters. She was the one I had been mocking in my room the day my mother gave me a bloody nose; I was making fun of the girl who was making fun of my sister. Elaine's father, Deacon Walters would get rewarded a few decades later for having established an excellent special education program. It would be far too late for Eileen who was out of school by then.

You could make a case for the dog being retarded, or at least defective in some way. Pal had not been neutered and was chained to his doghouse and neglected much of the time. He would frequently break the chain and run off looking for other dogs. He could jump through closed windows and screens and rummage through people's garbage looking for interesting stuff to eat or drag through the neighborhood.

My older brother had undiagnosed dyslexia and was slow to learn to read. He spent two years in first grade and saw a remedial reading teacher. I would learn to read quickly and read everything I could find. I liked school most of the time but was labeled a daydreamer who talked too much and looked out the window rather than completing my work.

Eileen attended school at the Gengras Center at St. Joseph's College until she was twenty-one years-old. Our local district, Simsbury Schools, granted a certificate of attendance. It was signed by Deacon Walters, who was still in the administration.

That year, 1976, Eileen began receiving SSI (Social Security Insurance). She got Medicaid and supportive services from the state. After leaving school, Eileen was provided transportation to a sheltered workshop where she could earn pocket money by doing various projects, being paid based on what an average person could accomplish in the same time. If the workshop had a contract to stuff envelopes or some other piece work, Eileen would get paid accordingly. There were also trips and recreational activities provided by the Department of Mental Retardation-Capitol region (DMRC), to make sure that handicapped people could participate in recreational and social events. After getting my driver's license, I was permitted to use the station wagon to drive Eileen to these activities.

During that time I volunteered with DMRC; they later changed their name to Association for Retarded Citizens (ARC). This would later be changed to "Arc" (the word, not the acronym) when the "R" word became unacceptable. I went through an orientation to be a volunteer. We referred to the adults in the program as "Clients." This provided them with as much dignity and respect as possible for people who lived in the bodies of adults but had the thinking capacity of young children.

There were some unexpected joys to working with this population. They have some of the innocence and excitability of children, but as adults they had lower energy levels, but also some unique skills and spots of wisdom. They were more varied and soulful than little children. They often knew how to enjoy and appreciate life in ways that still make me smile.

We took the clients bowling regularly. They were mostly terrible at bowling, but happy to be out in public. If they ever knocked any pins down at all, they celebrated like they had just won a jackpot. They didn't care about score-keeping or who won. They weren't upset or embarrassed when they got gutter-balls. I had never been bowling before working with handicapped adults. Later in life, when I tried bowling with typical adults, I found it to be depressing and dull by comparison.

One fun activity was a weekend trip to Washington DC. I had never been there, having missed the chance to go with my high school class because it cost more than I could afford. As a DMRC volunteer, I was able to go for free. All I had to do was make sure that the Clients didn't get lost.

I drove with Eileen to catch the charter bus, and we boarded before dawn on a Saturday morning. The seven-hour bus ride allowed me to get to know some of the other volunteers. I ate my bagged lunch with a man named Steve. He seemed interested in making friends with me. He was a nerdy mechanical engineer who was about thirty years-old and pleasant enough. Steve proudly showed me a brown paper lunch bag that he had regularly been using for several years. After eating his sandwich, he folded the bag neatly and tucked it in his shirt pocket.

Steve regaled me with his engineering knowledge. "If you knew how that bridge was constructed, you wouldn't want to ride this bus across it." He gave me detailed technical explanations of what made the bus likely to fall apart so drastically that we would all die. I found him tiresome, so after a while, I mingled with the Clients and other volunteers.

When we arrived in Washington DC, we had a pleasant time. We toured museums, had dinner, visited a park and then stayed in a hotel. Eileen and I shared a room. The next day we did a guided tour. The bus driver picked up a frightfully perky middle-aged tour guide, Mrs. Pepperton. She carried a bright red umbrella although it was not rainy. She told us to look for her umbrella if we got lost. She was an experienced tour guide, and it was apparent that she had been informed that she would be giving a tour to a group of mentally disabled people. It was also apparent that she was not comfortable with this group.

Her tour guide patter was delivered something like this: "And HERE you can see the WHITE marble dome of the JEFFERSON memorial. Thomas Jefferson was the THIRD president who wrote the DECLARATION of independence of the United States breaking AWAY from Great Britain. It SITS on the waters of the TIDAL basin, around which you can SEE the cherry blossom TREES which bloom at the CHERRY blossom festival EVERY spring. It's called the TIDAL basin because the POTOMAC River has tides that RESPOND to the pull of the MOON..." She repeated herself frequently and used a tone usually reserved for dogs.

When we left the bus for a walking tour, Mrs. Pepperton approached me as I was pushing one of the Clients in a wheelchair. She seemed uncomfortable talking to the Clients, and I was irritated with her condescending tone. She asked me if I was a volunteer. I didn't want to talk to her, so I looked at her, made a face and said "Huh" while scratching my head, hoping she would think I was one of the Clients; she looked horrified, and left me alone.

In spite of Mrs. Pepperton, a good time was had by all. We went back to the hotel, and all the Clients were put to bed. I went with some other volunteers and got drunk on whiskey and water in the bus driver's hotel room (Steve the engineer did not join us). A volunteer named Robert told a bad joke that involved someone eating turkey that had been sprayed by buckshot, and then fatally shooting his pet canary when he farted. I staggered back to Eileen's and my room and slept a few hours before rising early to ride the bus back home.

I was nursing a hangover when I sat with Steve. I told him that if he knew how much whiskey the bus driver had the night before he wouldn't feel safe. One of the Clients had purchased a whoopee cushion at a souvenir shop. Robert squeezed the whoopee cushion and shouted, "Someone just shot Mrs. Pepperton's canary!"

One time I drove Eileen to a dance for the local handicapped adults where my father would be playing drums with a band. I stayed and volunteered at the dance. A disabled young man who was reasonably nice looking followed me around and asked me to dance. I went with him to the dance floor where Eileen was standing and swaying to the music. I said, "Here, dance with my sister," and handed him off.

I saw Jack behind his drum set with his eyes tearing up. He had a vision of his oldest daughter looking like she had a good-looking boyfriend. This was something that would never happen, but he enjoyed seeing what it might look like.

The medical profession still had no specific classification for Eileen. She was different from most of the other crazy kids who talked, acted out, and got angry. Eileen would become silly, or frightened or withdrawn for unknown and unpredictable reasons. She would not learn to read or write beyond a second-grade level and never developed friendships with people. She attended school along with a mixed bunch of students loosely classified as emotionally disturbed or mentally retarded. The school was a bright spot of help, support, and compassion at a time when the local pillars of society in the schools and churches were dismissive.

Eileen would be in her thirties when a comprehensive evaluation finally identified it: Autism. This diagnosis was at odds with the evidence that she had been a bright and typical child until age four, if (according to Leo Kanner), Autism was innate. If she was normal and then regressed, then Bruno Bettelheim's refrigerator mom hypotheses might be a better fit. Because of the sudden regression, the vaccine theory Andrew Wakefield posed might have carried some weight, but Eileen did not have the Measles-Mumps-Rubella (MMR) Vaccination that Wakefield indicated. That vaccination wasn't yet available in the 1950s. The truth is there are still many things about Autism that we don't know. She was still going to sheltered workshop long after I graduated and went on my own way.

KITTY

Kitty in the cold

Kitty in the dark

Walking in the night

Then comes another kitty

And there are two

Walking in the night

Then comes morning

Run, run home kitty,

Kitty, kitty

-Eileen

Chapter 7
Intensive Care

Timmy was nearly ten years old and still had a leaking tube of scar tissue from his tracheotomy. It was time to have surgery so that he would be less susceptible to illness. He had learned to regulate the air pressure in his respiratory system so that he could swim. The doctor had trouble believing that was possible. He had also learned to talk when he was a baby by covering the stoma with his chin when he wanted to say a word or two. This was also unexpected by the medical professionals.

Timmy had his surgery in the spring when I was nineteen years old. I had a few weeks off in between college and summer camp, so I was helping out around the house and music store at that time. There were complications, and he ended up in intensive care, needing to stay in the hospital for a few days longer than anticipated.

He was unhappy about that. Ginny dropped me off at the hospital to spend the day and keep him company. Spring was at its most lovely, and the weather was warm and inviting. Timmy seemed to be recovering and able to do more than just lie in bed waiting to heal. After we both became bored with the available board games, we made our escape. I snuck Timmy out of the hospital and onto the streets of Hartford. We ate ice cream at a restaurant and then went to the top of a parking garage to spit on the sidewalks from nine or ten stories above. We were gone for hours and nobody back at the hospital even noticed.

A year or two after that, Timmy complained to me that Timmy was a baby name and Tim wasn't much better, and

Timothy was too long. I began calling him 'Mothy' or 'Moth' after that. Soon everyone else called him Tim. Our older brother had already shifted from Danny to Dan. I stayed Sharon and Eileen stayed Eileen.

Getting that Degree

Jack found a faded Volkswagen Karmann Ghia at a gas station. It wasn't running. The owner assumed the engine was shot, the fixing of which would cost more than the rusty car was worth. Jack bought it for $20. Dan changed the spark plugs and wires, and then it ran most of the time. It was ready just in time for me to finish my last year of college, which was to be my first year of college away from home.

It was my first car. There was a short circuit in it that quickly drained the battery. After being parked for a few hours, the car wouldn't start. Fixing that would require paying a mechanic money, and that would never do, so Jack figured out some workarounds. I could, each time I parked, lift the hood and disconnect the battery. Or, I could park it on a hill and start it by rolling it down the hill, turning the ignition and popping the clutch.

Connecticut had a loophole in car safety at the time. If you purchased a used car that was less than ten years old, you didn't need a safety inspection to get it registered. It was possible to get a car for $100 that was close to ten years old, which had no chance of passing safety and emission checks. If you could make minor repairs yourself, you might get six months or a year's use out of them. If it still ran but needed significant repairs, like a new exhaust system that was worth more than the car, you could decide to drive them to the junkyard, turn over the title and get $50. If the vehicle could not be driven to the junkyard, the junk dealer would deduct the cost of towing the car and pay you $25. A series of these forlorn vehicles got me through college, and my first attempt at graduate school.

The summer before I went away to my last year of college, I was back at Lenox Hill Camp. That's where I met Jon. Ours was an odd relationship. He lived near where I grew up. I was twenty, and Jon was twenty-five when we met. He had not settled down in a career.

Jon was brilliant but unable to decide what to do with his life. He dreamed of being a pediatrician but never lasted more than a semester in college before leaving for some reason. He smoked cigarettes all the time and had an alcohol problem that didn't seem so problematic to me at the time. My parents were heavy drinkers who got drunk sometimes but never escalated their drinking to the degree that it interfered with their health or work.

Jon and I hit it off immediately, but he was involved with a long-time girlfriend, and so we just became good friends and drinking buddies. We spent every spare minute hanging out together and had long deep conversations. Everyone at camp assumed we were lovers, and in every way (except physically) we were intimately involved.

Eastern Connecticut State College accepted all of my credits. It looked like I would be able to complete the rest of my bachelor's degree courses in one year. I was able to secure a $1,500 loan, and with my savings, I could finance that year without having to work during the school year.

I needed physical education credits, so I took a lifeguard class. This class led to a part-time job offer at the local YMCA. The idea of being paid to sit by a pool for 15 hours each week was irresistible. So I worked through my last year of college and could enjoy occasional beers or pizzas.

Jack was still working on getting the Karmann Ghia running, so it was Ginny who drove me to the ECSC campus about one hour east of Tariffville, to register and find a place to live. It was cheaper to rent off campus in Willimantic than to live on campus in a dormitory. The old mill town near the school was crumbling; the primary employer, a thread factory had just recently closed. The locals had no more union jobs, and the town was emptying out. The old homes were being converted into off-campus rentals. I rented a room with a mini-fridge and hot plate on the second floor of a Victorian house. I spent a lot of my time studying. I drove my little Karmann Ghia home some weekends to do my laundry and pick up things I needed from my old room. Not much fits in a Karmann Ghia. The back seat was only spacious enough for small children, and the trunk could hold little more than a briefcase.

When I started my year in Willimantic, I was missing Jon. When camp ended, he had gone back to his job at the Capitol Region Educational Center, a residential school for children we referred to as CREC. He also went back to his girlfriend, Cindy. I tried to forget him and focus on my studies. This was working until he decided to show up in my little college town and rent an apartment in the same building where I was living. He said it was because it was cheap and a reasonable commuting distance to CREC. His relationship with Cindy had ended, but nothing changed with me.

The kids at CREC had behavior problems that their families couldn't deal with in a day program. They had a strict behavioral modification program. The facility included a small indoor swimming pool. By spring I had a job some evenings and weekends running that swimming pool and helping out with after-school activities.

I was a few credits short of my BA when the spring semester ended, so I took another CLEP exam and an accelerated three-week class that I could just barely squeeze between the end of the spring semester and when summer camp started. Willimantic and Lenox Hill Camp were both an hour from Tariffville but in different directions. I needed to spend a weekend at the camp in Litchfield for staff orientation, drive two hours back to college, take the final exam on Monday and be back at camp Tuesday when the campers were to arrive.

I left camp at 10:00 Sunday night. There were few open gas stations on the way, and I suspected my tank was low. The Karmann Ghia didn't have a working speedometer or gas gauge, and one headlight had stopped working. A friend once told me that there were usually a few ounces of gas in the hoses at gas stations, and Volkswagens got such good mileage I might be able to make it by stopping and draining the dregs from each hose at each gas station I passed into my gas tank. I also shut off the engine and coasted down hills, and jump-started as I reached the bottom of each hill.

I was doing ok, but I ran out of gas as I neared Hartford close to midnight. A friendly cop gave me a lift to a gas station. I kept a three-gallon gas can in the car for such occasions. I was afraid I'd get a ticket when the cop saw that one headlight was not working. He ignored it and waved me on. I slept a few hours at the apartment, took the final exam and drove back to camp.

Then I worked thirteen-hour days all summer, commuting back and forth to my apartment in Willimantic. I should explain why I maintained that apartment. After all, I was only there to finish college, and it was nowhere near my home or my job. The camp was where I slept except for maybe three days that summer. There were a couple of reasons I kept the apartment. First of all, it was very inexpensive, still only $34 a month. Second, Jon was keeping his apartment in the same building, and since we worked in the same places, we could drive together. Jon thought it was a good idea, and I went along with it. Everyone thought we were lovers and it was easier to maintain the illusion than explain the situation that I had trouble understanding myself. It was not the best decision I ever made.

In retrospect, that relationship was wrong for me. Jon was depressed and addicted to alcohol and nicotine. He was cynical and found reasons to find fault with jobs, bosses, and institutions. But Jon was kind to me and treated me with respect. He echoed a libertarian sense of independence that I didn't realize fit with the ethos I had been raised with. I didn't see this parallel because he was young, irreverent and shaggy-haired. This characteristic was probably what gave me the sense when we first met that I had known him all my life.

Although I had known since I started college that my goal was to get to graduate school as soon as possible, I was unaware of the need to take the GRE in December of the previous year. Since I lived off campus as a senior and had earned most of my credits at a two-year school, I hadn't spent much time with the sorts of students and professors who talked about graduate school plans. I didn't learn about the GRE until it was too late to take it. I would have to wait another year for graduate school.

I was able to accept this development because I was running out of money and realized that working full time for a year would enable me to save up. Also, in my haste to earn my undergraduate degree as quickly and cheaply as possible, I had not explored my options with graduate programs. And, I was in love with Jon.

Break from School

After I completed my undergraduate credits, Jon and I went back to working at Lenox Hill Camp. Once again we appeared to be a couple. Jon even made comments in public that suggested we were lovers. I was unable to define what was going on between Jon and me. I loved him, he seemed to love me, we were best friends, and we were as emotionally intimate are people can be. I was frustrated, embarrassed, and too confused to confide in anyone.

My parents had met Jon, liked him and assumed we were in a serious romantic relationship. They were furious when I told them that Jon and I were sharing an apartment. They called it "shacking up" spitting those words at me. There was no point in telling them we weren't sexually involved—they wouldn't have believed me.

Jon smoked cigarettes and drank every evening we spent together. I drank at about half his pace and noticed after a while that my tolerance for booze was going up. I was usually a lightweight who would feel the effects of one or two drinks. I was up to three or more drinks and still able to work and get good grades. Since I needed to take a year off school and take the GRE, I had to find a job. Jon and I applied and were hired to be co-house parents at Oak Hill School in Hartford.

It had been a residential school for blind children that served the entire Northeastern United States, in the days when the handicapped children were usually sent to specialized schools. Beginning in 1974, new laws required disabled students to be educated in the least restrictive environment. Students who were blind or deaf could now attend their local districts. Oak Hill School was transitioning from a campus for children who were only blind to a school that met the needs of students who were blind and handicapped in other ways as well.

Oak Hill School wanted to move the higher functioning kids into group homes off campus, while the dorms would be filled with more severely disabled children. High school students, who had been at Oak Hill since they were very young, were allowed to stay until they graduated even if they were only blind and not handicapped in additional ways. These kids were scheduled to move with Jon and me into a house near the campus, whenever that house became ready. Jon and I would then live there with the kids to take care of them before and after school.

I expected to attend graduate school while the Oak Hill kids went to their classes. I looked forward to free room and board with pay as an ideal way to support myself in school. There were some fascinating things about the kids at Oak Hill. We arranged dances for the teenagers. When the music stopped, the blind kids stopped dancing, and the deaf kids continued dancing. The staff tried very hard not to laugh.

I brought my guitar to evening shifts and played and sang for an hour each evening at bedtime. The kids enjoyed my singing, and the staff enjoyed the calming distraction my folk-rock music provided. The kids learned the songs I played regularly and requested their favorites. I sang Both Sides Now, Someday Soon, and Different Drum. Some of the kids rocked back and forth as a way to deal with sensory issues. When they rocked themselves to my music, they seemed less unusual.

Jon and I had worked split shifts in the Oak Hill dorms until the off-campus house renovations were complete. While we waited for the home to be ready, we were still living in Willimantic. We commuted twice a day before and after school hours. We woke up at 6:00, got in a car at 6:20, commuted forty minutes, and then took care of the kids for two hours from 7-9:00. The kids were in school for six hours. During that time we would commute back, rest, and return to school at 3:00 and work until 9:00.

The Karmann Ghia had stopped running. I gave it to Timmy for Christmas. He was 12 years old and so excited to get a car. He was able to clean it up and sell it for $100. Jon's brother Alan had a car he wanted to sell. Although it was banged up and leaking oil, it was running. So for $100, I became the owner of a 1972 Oldsmobile Delta 88.

It had been a luxury car. It had silk-brocade seats that were no longer white but stained. The front seat was broken, braced in place with a pine two-by-four wedged between it and the back seat. The front grille was held in place with wire. It was running a little rough and needed new points and spark plugs. After turning over the title, Alan told me there were new points in the glove compartment (The points were the part of the engine that regulated the charge helped the cylinders fired in sequence).

There was one delay after another in getting the live-in group home ready. The hours, the drinking, and the disappointment of the group home situation began to take a toll on me and on my relationship with Jon. I wanted to hold onto the house parent job so that I could attend graduate school while being paid to live as a caretaker. Jon was hoping to become a stable adult with more of a career.

180

Jon went back to a slightly better job at CREC. I stayed at Oak Hill, doing both my job and Jon's as well. I realized it was actually easier to work without Jon, because he had been draining my energy with his cynical attitude and bad habits. It made little sense for me to stay in Willimantic; the commute was killing me, and Jon was no longer even helpful for carpooling. I moved back in with my parents. Jon, who for over a year had been giving people the false impression we were a couple, now acted like I had broken up with him.

I had to pay my parents $100 each month for room and board. This was the deal they made for Dan and me unless we were full-time students. The commute from Tariffville was easier. I had a task that I needed to complete, and that was to arrange to get the bachelor's degree I had earned but not been awarded. I took off my morning shift off on a regular workday instead and drove to Willimantic to do whatever was needed to get my degree.

Getting through the process was a bureaucratic nightmare. I wasn't currently enrolled, so I had to apply again. I couldn't apply yet because I had neither dropped out nor been asked to leave, and I couldn't re-enroll because I never withdrew. I had to go all the way to the Dean, who had to call the college president. But I went out with the dean's assurance I would get my degree.

That task completed, I returned to the parking lot to find that my Oldsmobile Delta 88 wouldn't start. It had been running worse and worse, and I figured it needed the new points sitting in the glove compartment. I kept a toolbox in the trunk and replaced the points. That seemed to do the trick. The car started up, and I returned to Oak Hill School, about 45 minutes away. The ride back was interesting. I didn't want to be late for my afternoon shift, so even though the engine began balking, speeding up, slowing down, and not responding normally to the gas pedal, I kept driving. By the time I got to work, it sounded like it was vomiting. When I turned off the ignition, it coughed and wheezed a bit before shutting down.

The next day I called and told Jack that I needed help with my car. It wasn't going to start without some help. He came that Saturday in his Jeep Cherokee with a tow rope if needed. Tim came along for the ride. He was always up for a trip. With some tinkering, we got the Oldsmobile sputtering but running. Jack decided to drive it to his garage to work on it. Tim and I followed in the Jeep. My car was barely able to move at a reasonable speed. I was worried and gripping the steering wheel white-knuckled hoping that my means of freedom and income was repairable. All of a sudden, BANG! The muffler exploded causing the 4300-pound sedan to lift clear off the road. Even still, it kept running. Jack kept driving, and Tim and I laughed so hard we almost cried.

It turns out the points were not the right ones for the car. After a tune-up and a trip to the muffler shop (where they refused to replace the muffler until I assured them that whatever caused the explosion that left the original muffler in shreds had been repaired), this $100 car was beginning to cost me as much as a better car.

I took the GRE. When it looked like Oak Hill was never going to get the group home ready for my residential position, I got a job working at a different group home nearby. This one provided for disabled adults and I worked as many shifts as I could. Saving up my money, I applied to a graduate program at the University of Hartford.

In the spring, as I passed my twenty-second birthday, I got accepted into the clinical psychology master's degree program. They regularly took 15 out of 300 applicants. I had done well on the GRE, and my GPA was high enough.

I didn't want to attend full time because I was no longer in such a hurry to finish school. I didn't feel prepared to deal with a full course load while working part-time and I didn't have enough money saved up to complete the two-year program. I didn't realize that the grants that would have paid for my undergraduate education were not available for graduate school. Now that I was able to apply without a parent signature, I was too well-educated. I was tired of working all the time and saving every penny for school. I wanted to have a life, to be able to buy myself some decent clothes. I had gotten skinnier, and my shabby clothes were hanging on me.

When I asked about taking two classes each semester, they told me no. So I decide to go full time in the fall. I had saved up $10,000 during my year off from school. That was only enough to pay for the first year. The maximum I could borrow for graduate school with government subsidized loans was $5,000. I borrowed the maximum and put the money away to save for the second year.

I prepared that summer by getting my Delta 88 fixed. I replaced the head gasket myself in the driveway. I paid for parts and got some major repairs done at a local school for car mechanics. I fixed up an old ten-speed bike that a neighbor had thrown away for riding to work when my car was being repaired.

I prided myself on finding ways to get things done on the cheap as I was raised to do. The mechanic school didn't charge for labor, but they kept my car for a week. When my car was at the mechanic school, I rode the ten-speed to work and back. By the time school started that Fall, I would be ready. I was driving a car that I purchased for $100. It had new brakes, a tune-up and new head gasket and new tires.

The group home job let me switch to a part-time position that fit my class schedule. Each morning I would wake the Clients, make them breakfast, drive them to the workshop where they spent the day, and clean the kitchen and bathrooms. That being done, I would be ready to start classes.

My car was reliable. I was renting a room in an apartment with two roommates in between my job and the campus. I was ready to dive into the demands of full-time graduate school. Just a few days before classes were to start; I was driving the twisty road near my parent's house when a girl in a Toyota crossed the center line. I caught the sight of her face; I could see her panicked expression and indecision about which way to go—back to her side of the road or all the way across where there was a relatively flat, treeless area. I stood on my brake pedal and left a perfectly straight skid for about 20 feet and then saw her car hit the front of my car and bounce off. The Toyota rolled a few times, and a man stopped to direct traffic around my wrecked car.

A 1972 Delta 88 was a good car for a head-on collision. The big eight-cylinder engine absorbed the shock of the crash, and the renovated brakes held steady. I came out with a bruise on my knee and a bump on my head. I wasn't wearing a seatbelt. The girl in the Toyota wasn't either. She crawled out, bruised all over but apparently nothing was broken. Both cars were totaled. I got some insurance money: three or four hundred dollars. The girl was seventeen years-old and married. She was on her way to a job interview and was driving a rented car. She and her husband were in deep trouble. Me? I just needed another vehicle.

Graduate School

I arrived at graduate school a little shaken up from the car accident. When meeting my classmates, I found I was the youngest one there, with the least education. I had attended the cheapest schools. I was one of fifteen first-year students in the program. There were only five second-year students. We asked the second year students "What happened to the rest of your class?" The answer was: they too had started out with fifteen and were now down to five. The class ahead of them had graduated only three. On top of this, the University of Hartford psychology grad program was converting from a Masters to a PhD program and was in the process of being evaluated by a credentialing board. I was in over my head.

I also found out that two of my classmates had made the same request I had about attending part-time. They were initially told no like I was, but when they refused to go full time, they were permitted to take two classes at a time.

Then there were the classes. Behavioral Techniques was an interesting class. I had a solid foundation for this from my undergraduate programs. I was not happy with the idea that human behavior could be reduced to stimulus and response, but at least it was grounded in science and data. The professor was one of the kindest and warmest instructors in the program.

The counseling class was fun but weird. We practiced counseling each other. We watched as second-year students acted out various mental disorders with a counselor, while we observed from behind a one-way mirror. We then discussed what kind of neurosis or psychosis was being acted out. In one session, a student-actor was thrashing his hands about in front of his face. We all decided he was hallucinating because we couldn't see through the mirror that a horsefly was tormenting him.

My best subject was intelligence testing. As I was living close to home, I was able to test my brothers and Jack. They had similar strengths and weaknesses as very bright but dyslexic people. I obtained results that gave me some definite ideas about how to use testing as a tool.

Ginny refused to take the IQ test. She was worried that I might find out that she was not as smart as she pretended to be. I suspect she believed her success in school was due to her memory and hard work rather than ability. She studied languages and learned bookkeeping for the businesses, but admitted to not being able to understand science fiction. She may have had difficulty with abstract ideas, compensating by memorizing more facts and data than most. Jack, on the other hand, was quick with words, humor, and creative problem-solving, but not so good with details. The two of them may have been entirely complementary, functioning better as one brain when they went into business together.

The personality class was another story. We had to give Rorschach tests and other projective tests, and then make assumptions about people's inner lives based on symbolism. I was reluctant to label people based on such flimsy information. A second-year student assigned to help me said, "Use your imagination" when I balked at writing a thorough analysis of test subjects' reactions to ink blots and ambiguous pictures. I was not comfortable fabricating results to enhance my grades. Some of my classmates seemed okay with it.

We observed how one professor suggested countless ways to detect latent homosexuality; we surmised that many of these indicators probably applied to him.

I tried to conceal my honest doubts and questions regarding some of the diagnostic techniques and the subjective nature of the assessments. I was on a search for truth and found myself being encouraged to replace legitimate uncertainty with false certainty. I envied the section of neuropsychology/physiology students in a program that paralleled ours. It seemed to me that the answers to questions regarding people like my sister were in chemistry and neurology, but I didn't have the hard science background for that program.

While I was struggling in school, my new roommates were using drugs more and more. I began jogging. It worked well for managing the stress and helped me reconnect with my body after ignoring physical needs for so long. It was beginning to look like when my class became second-year students, I would be one of the reasons the next set of first-year students had to ask "What happened to the rest of your class?"

Meanwhile, in the real world, the Shah of Iran was sent packing in exile to the United States. When I visited my parent's house, I found the television turned to the news. I saw crowds of men in Iran protesting. I wondered what was happening. I couldn't remember learning anything about this country in history class. I looked it up and realized it was Persia, where the rich, black-haired guys at my community college came from. I remembered Mokar, with the long hair and a shaggy beard, who told me he didn't want to go back. He was Americanized. His fellow Iranian students dressed like pimps and enjoyed the company of women—and getting drunk or high.

The insurgents on the TV news took the Americans at the embassy hostage. I heard that all Persians in the U.S. were going to be deported because it was an act of war. It looked like World War III was about to start. One of my roommates was selling cocaine and pot. To top it off, my grades were not good enough for me to continue with school. I decided to take some time off from school and look for a professional-level job. I checked out a few manager jobs at residential homes for homeless youths but found myself drawn to the military recruiting station.

With a bachelor's degree, I could proceed directly into officer training. The Air Force had excellent options for women and fewer restrictions as to where they could serve. But the Navy had recently begun allowing women to serve on ships. Plus, the Navy had more appealing locations in warmer climates.

I was in the process of formally withdrawing from graduate school and arranging to sell some of my books to one of the part-time students when I was asked to meet with the professors in the clinical psychology program. They were very kind about telling me I wasn't ready for the program. I reminded them that I wanted to go part-time and they had not granted that option to me. They had some suggestions about other programs that I might do better in and told me that I could expect excellent letters of recommendation for jobs or other graduate programs. I replied that I was planning to join the Navy.

Some professors were shocked and worried that I'd gone off the deep end. But two Navy veteran students in my class wished me well and assured me it was a wise move. The behavioral studies teacher was enthusiastically supportive and told me how much he enjoyed my questions in class. He said I was a good student and should try school again.

Over the years when looking for ways to help pay for my education, I had considered the ROTC (Reserve Officer Training Corps) program a few times but passed on that option because of the five-year military service commitment that had to be completed before I could attend graduate school. I considered that too long a wait. Now here I was, about to sign up for a minimum four years of not being able to go to graduate school. I could have had my undergraduate education paid for if I had more foresight.

I signed the no-turning-back agreement and raised my right hand to take the military oath a few days after a helicopter crashed in the desert on a rescue mission to Iran. Ginny asked me if I still wanted to go through with it after this embarrassing failure, but I was sure. I needed to get away from human services for a while, have a professional-level job and see what else I could do. I expected to return to human services someday, probably psychology, but as an older, wiser and more capable person. I had seen social workers and psychologists in the various agencies I worked in struggle to get things done because of bureaucracy and regulations. The military seemed to be an excellent place to learn about managing red tape and organizational constraints. I figured that experience with a vast bureaucratic machine would be something valuable I could bring to whatever position I might eventually hold.

While I waited for my departure to Navy Officer Candidate School (OCS), I bumped into Ricky Rooney, former bus driver. We had coffee in a diner and chatted about our lives in the six years since we had been together. He asked what I was up to and I told him I was joining the Navy in a few weeks. He said, "Oh no, that's bad Karma."

Ricky had quit smoking but instead looking healthier he looked very thin and pale, twitchy and paranoid. He told me he was worried about being followed. He had recently left the Church of Scientology and believed they were following him. Since I had researched Scientology, I was able to understand and corroborate some of his story.

He said he had been a recruiter for the church. This I could believe. I knew that they used good-looking people to lure in new members. He believed that high-level members had supernatural powers and would punish him if they found him. His hushed voice and frequent scanning of the diner indicated he wasn't making this up.

Ricky's story confirmed my suspicions of Scientology, and I wondered if his general flakiness and immaturity made him more vulnerable to the coercive techniques of a mind-control cult. I wondered how safe I was from falling prey to a cult. I was still an open-minded adventurer, but I was wary of the possibilities of mind control. Little did I realize that it would take decades for me to escape the programming of my parents.

I had pledged an oath to protect and serve the Constitution of the United States, but I vowed to myself to keep my mind free from the power of authority, faith, and charismatic leaders.

"Holy Shit! They Aren't Kidding!"

I, Sharon Hogan, do solemnly swear that I will support and defend the Constitution of the United States against all enemies, foreign and domestic; that I will bear true faith and allegiance to the same; and that I will obey the orders of the President of the United States and the orders of the officers appointed over me, according to regulations and the Uniform Code of Military Justice. So help me God.

I passed the months leading up to OCS continuing to be active at the group home and working out as much as I could. I was fit and healthy. The recruiting slogan at the time read: Navy. It's not just a job, it's an adventure. I had no idea of what I was getting myself into, but I was up for the adventure.

I checked into OCS on a windy Sunday afternoon, wearing sandals and a tee-shirt dress. I was carrying my guitar and a suitcase containing a few articles of clothes, all of my underwear and some good running shoes.

A tall man in a khaki uniform verified my paperwork and took my suitcase. He was brusque in his instructions. "Follow me. Walk four inches from the bulkhead (that's the wall). Cage your eyes (that means look straight ahead, not up not down not to the side). When you turn left or right square your corners." Then he demonstrated how to pivot on one foot to make a 90-degree turn.

I followed him into King Hall, the vast red brick building that housed up to 1,000 people. I was wondering if this walking 4 inches from the wall and squaring the corners were going to be my life for the next four months, finding the idea unbelievable and a little bit funny.

As I followed the man holding my suitcase, I didn't cage my eyes. I looked around furtively. When we got to the end of one hall, he pivoted in the corner, and I noticed that on the spot he lifted his heel from, there was a circle on the floor where the tile was nearly worn through from the pivoting shoes of thousands of officer candidates. Holy Shit! I thought to myself. He really meant it. What have I gotten myself into? This is like a prison.

Officer Candidate School in Newport, Rhode Island, became gender integrated in 1978. I arrived in May of 1980. The adjustments of women having the same training as men were still being worked out. There were about 500 men and 100 women in my class. Within a few weeks, our numbers shrank as people realized they weren't cut out for military training or were found to be unable to function under the rigid demands of military training. A few were found unable to pass security clearance background checks, and they too were sent home.

I wasn't used to this kind of regimented educational experience, but I was well prepared for the physical demands. Marching, however, was difficult for me. My lifetime of daydreaming while on long walks coupled with my unusually flexible joints made me very sloppy in formation. Being female, with a swing in my step, didn't help matters. I was so inept at marching the leaders of our company made me the photographer when the time came for marching competition between companies.

I could shine my shoes and press my uniform as well as anyone. The female uniform was cut differently than the men's. All of us women received lower marks on uniform inspections because our curved bodies, and the fact that our uniforms buttoned and zipped right over left instead of left over right made us look wrong to the inspecting officers.

I struggled with some of the academics. There was a lot of math and memorization. I was not good at concentrating on detailed minutiae regarding regulations. I was unprepared for the mathematical calculations required for celestial navigation and a subject called maneuvering aboard. This required calculating speed and direction of ships to avoid collisions. I needed help learning these subjects.

We were required to participate each Saturday in inter-company competition. We called it "Mandatory Fun." Here I was an asset to my company. There were 50 men and seven women in my company, and each team was required to have at least one woman. I wasn't a swift runner, but I could run all out for the quarter mile and keep our team from losing ground. The men and women in my company knew I was the weakest member of the relay team so they cheered me on as loudly as they could, and we would win the relay race every week. Then I became the secret weapon on the water polo team. I was a good swimmer with endurance in the water. Being female, I was also more buoyant than a man and needed less energy to tread water for an entire match. I was not good at catching or throwing the ball, but I could block the best players on any other company team.

Besides preparing new officers for ship driving, damage control, and discipline administration, OCS gave us essential training in such crucial areas as removing all detectable dust from urinals in the women's bathrooms. We also learned trash cans should not have trash in them, and that the enemy would defeat us if our bound publications were not stacked and ordered precisely on our shelves.

I am not proud to admit that I graduated last in my class, but I was ahead of the nearly 100 out of the original 600 who dropped out by request, flunked out, or were required to repeat the whole 16 weeks of training. It was a considerably better success rate than my graduate school program, it turns out. The ones who started it and didn't finish were called DE's, "disenrolled." The repeaters were called "roll-backs." I was called an Ensign.

My whole family came to my graduation, and we posed for family photos against the Narragansett Bay, not far from the waters where the family used to go boating.

See the World

I hoped to get sea duty and serve on a ship. The Navy had only recently begun allowing women to serve on ships. When I completed OCS and got my commission, there were four openings for women officers on ships. They went to the first female Academy graduates. Career patterns were set up so if a woman did not go to sea as a new ensign, she never would. I would do nothing but shore duty.

My first duty station was Guam. I acquired a lot of responsibility and management experience while living out my childhood tropical island fantasy. I had some short-term romantic relationships there.

The military transfers people frequently, so the system is set up to function without any particular person is indispensable. I found myself assigned to a series of increasingly responsible jobs. I managed divisions and departments of 15-to-60 personnel. Eventually, I controlled an annual budget of over a million dollars. I took advantage of something called space-available travel. I could fly for free on military aircraft if there was space. It might be a seat, a place on the cargo deck or a canvass bench strapped to the side of a cargo plane. I traveled to Japan, Korea, and the Philippine Islands in this way.

I got mail from my parents back in the states. They included photographs of houses in the New London area, where they were getting ready to move. There was a man I did not know in these pictures. After seeing him in several pictures, I looked closer and recognized my father. I was surprised to find out it was him. He had been diagnosed with diabetes, and to avoid needles he had radically altered his diet and exercise habits, and he lost so much weight he was nearly unrecognizable.

After a year on the small island in the Pacific, I found myself stationed at a small base on the Potomac River. I was able to buy a small house in Dahlgren, Virginia, using savings and unused graduate school student loan money for the down payment.

I had pretty much forgiven my parents as I spent more time living far away from them. We exchanged cheerful, newsy letters and phone calls. I initiated most of the contact and, now that I was back in the states, visited once or twice a year. There was a period of peace and positive relations between us.

Shortly after I returned from overseas, they moved from the house where I grew up to their dream home on Niantic Bay. They had benefitted from some real estate sales and experienced a period of financial prosperity. Tim was healthy, and Eileen had settled into a quietly withdrawn routine. She went to a sheltered workshop during weekdays and spent all of her free time creating her art. Ginny did Eileen's laundry, cleaned up after her, and packed her lunch each day.

During those years I lived with or near my parents, I had observed Eileen's behavior regularly. Eileen was quiet and kept to herself. She would come to breakfast and dinner when called and could make her own lunch on weekends. Ginny would still supervise her weekly bath and hair washing and insisted that Eileen ask for help whenever she wanted to heat leftovers or a beverage in the microwave oven. Ginny was often in the basement office attending to business, leaving Eileen free to do as she wished on the main floor of the house or retreat to her upstairs bedroom in the addition.

I tried to encourage my mother to teach Eileen to be more independent. I told her how we worked with clients at the group home, teaching them how to take care of their own clothes and personal hygiene.

Ginny wouldn't consider letting Eileen wash her own hair or learn to be independent in any way. Eileen sat passively in the bathtub during her weekly bath, waiting for Ginny to come in and take care of her hair, just like when we were toddlers. She claimed to be worried that Eileen wouldn't rinse her hair properly. I knew from work experience and from teaching Eileen how to follow directions in the kitchen that she could be trained to do this. Eileen was passive and allowed Ginny to manage her. Although I had education and experience in this area, arguing was futile. Ginny would not consider allowing Eileen to learn to be independent in any way.

The new dream house fit my parent's desires and lifestyle. In the summer of 1982, they had the prefabricated sections of their modular home placed on the foundation on the waterfront lot. They added a passive solar greenhouse and built a room that connected the two-car garage to the main house. This external room would become the office for their scaled-down business activities. It was the front entrance to the house as well.

After they settled in, Ginny, at last, had her dream house with its dream kitchen. She chose all the decor and furnishings. She landscaped the yard and planted flower and vegetable beds. They had sold off all of their Simsbury rental properties and became semi-retired. Jack would still swing a few more real estate deals, but mostly he spent most of his days playing with their golden retriever Trevor, and puttering with projects like fixing up old boats and collecting cast-off junk that might be useful for some future project. Jack filled the massive garage with scrap lumber and found items. Soon the only thing that exited the garage regularly was the lawn mower.

Eileen was twenty-seven years old when they moved. Ginny's letters to experts and the psychiatric reports from that time indicated that after the move Eileen had regressed and shown signs of obsessive-compulsive disorder (OCD). She pulled out most of her eyelashes. Ginny began seeking help and treatment for Eileen. She researched OCD and various therapies. She took Eileen to experts at The University of Connecticut and Yale.

I called them every few weeks during this time, and Ginny would update me on Eileen's behavior and her search for treatments. Eileen was becoming more of a problem, Ginny said. She would stay up late and dawdle over meals. Ginny would wake her each morning, and Eileen would stay in bed and go back to sleep. Eileen became stubborn. Her previously passive cooperation became passive-aggressive. In response, Ginny grew shrill and demanding.

This was the pre-internet era. In her search for control methods, Ginny went to libraries and attended talks by experts at colleges. It was soon apparent that Eileen required a diagnosis. Psychiatrists prescribed Haldol (Haloperidol) and Anafranil (Clomipramine). Eileen's behaviors didn't change very much, but she finally had a diagnosis: Autism. With this diagnosis in hand, Ginny had a new subject to research. She was soon able to present herself as an expert to the social workers provided by the state.

Eileen was immune to coercion, medication and behavioral techniques. All the time I was growing up, the usual parenting techniques of spanking, yelling and threatening didn't work on Eileen. Fortunately for my parents, Eileen was passive and usually went along with routines, in her quiet, slow way. She had only required a bit more time and patience to comply with demands to get dressed, get ready to go somewhere, or come to dinner.

At about this time Trevor had developed a habit of licking the top of his front paws until the fur began to disappear. Golden retrievers are genetically prone to obsessive behavior. Soon Eileen and Trevor were both taking Anafranil—a relatively new treatment for OCD. Trevor responded better to this medication than Eileen did.

Autism V

Doctors do not possess perfect knowledge. Armed with the DSM, they can diagnose a child with Autism, but that does not make them experts on everything about it. There remain aspects of the disorder that nobody can explain.

It is absurd to tell a parent their child was born Autistic and they managed not to notice. Any parent will notice something as dramatic as a baby who will not interact the way other babies do. The phenomenon of Autism developing after a period of normal development is considered rare by the experts, but perhaps this happens more frequently than has been believed.

Sometimes a three year-old who will develop Autism will have behavior indistinguishable from a three year-old who goes on to live a healthy life. This is because Autism can be triggered sometime in the preschool years. The mechanism by which the trigger starts the Autism is still unknown.

Because of the mysterious nature of the brain itself, and since often not enough attention was paid to early behaviors by parents reporting a sudden change in their child's behavior, there were few reliable answers for parents asking "what happened to my child?" This set the stage in 1997 for the hoax and false claims made by Andrew Wakefield. Wakefield published an article based on false data that vaccinations caused Autism.

People were hungry for an explanation for the drastic increase in the rate of Autism after 1980. The real reason was that the diagnosis was not widely known or available until that time. All the people like Eileen who had Autism for years were finally being identified. Many children who were thought of as odd but not fitting into any psychological category were being labeled with Autism or Asperger's Syndrome.

Parents don't want to believe a misfortune befalling their child "just happened." They want to blame someone or something. They want to know if some triggering event could have been avoided. Searching for such a cause, they would think back to what may have brought on their child's sudden regression.

Because the onset of Autism tends to occur, or be noticed in the preschool years, it is likely that the most recent encounter with medicine was a vaccination. Parents desperate for answers naturally grab onto any available explanation, including the fallacy that vaccinations cause Autism.

Andrew Wakefield blamed Autism on the Measles-Mumps-Rubella (MMR) vaccine, which contained a trace of the preservative thimerisol (a form of mercury), which in large quantities acts as a neurotoxin. His work was debunked over and over by the scientific community. His research data was found to be fraudulent and his conclusions unsupportable. There was evidence that he expected to sell a different vaccine which would have made him rich if he could damage the reputations of the owners of vaccines required across much of the world. Nevertheless, his imaginary link between Autism and vaccines was taken up by celebrities and worried parents, and continues until the present (Jonathan D. Quick, MD MPH and Heidi Larson, "The Vaccine-Autism Myth Started 20 years Ago. Here's Why it Still Endures Today." Time Magazine [February 28, 2018]).

In the 1950's there was no MMR vaccine to blame. Children who acted oddly, failed to develop normally, or had a sudden regression after a period of normal development

were labeled with mental retardation, childhood schizophrenia or something completely unrelated. Many of these
children were assumed to have been abused, spoiled, or
dropped on their heads.

RAIN

Rain like water drops

Water drops out of the sky

But I know the difference about them

It is for secret weapons I will know and I will keep

Raindrops tell a story

Some are over the trees where my love has found them

My love knows where it can fall

Somewhere someone knows what love is being.

The bus knows that too I go on a trip to raindrop land

I know everything in raindrop land — and then I want to go home

But home I have to use an umbrella.

-Eileen

Chapter 8
Lost Baby

I did not fit in with the local Dahlgren rednecks, who told me I was a Yankee or a Damned Yankee if I told them I didn't find their openly racist statements acceptable. If I engaged them in discussions regarding equality of all people they said I was ignorant and assured me that black people were happier with the overt racism of the South than they were with the more subtle racism of the North. Most of the Navy personnel stationed at this small Virginia weapons testing facility were older than me and married.

I was lonely for literate, progressive company so I joined a dating service, hoping to find some friends I could relate to. I met Carlos near the end of December 1982. We were engaged to be married within seven weeks, although neither of us had specified marriage as a wish on the dating service application form.

Carlos was already considering a military career when we met, as a way to develop the kind of résumé that would help him get a government job like his father's. He was a talented musician; however, he had decided on a stable career that could better provide him with the money and security to have music as a hobby, rather than trying to make a living by playing music. Shortly after we got engaged, he enlisted in the Navy and was scheduled for OCS in Newport Rhode Island, as I had done three years before.

The Navy gave me a chance to prove I could do a man's job, earn the same money and status as a man. I was also interested in having fun, traveling, and being an independent young adult. After struggling to work my way through college, the junior officer pay and benefits and responsibilities made me feel more powerfully in control of my life than I had felt as a civilian. In comparison to the way we scrimped and saved when I was growing up and working my way through college, as a junior officer I felt rich.

I saw my military experience as an adventure, a chance to prove myself and learn to function as a leader. My parents saw it differently; they took my Navy career decision as a sign that I had become a conservative Republican. They had eased up on me when I cut my bushy hair short at age twenty. They were thrilled and proud of my military service. hadn't changed my views but began keeping them to myself, letting my parents assume I was on their side. I remained a moderate, open-minded feminist.

The brief period of improved relations with my parents ended when I got married. They disliked my husband from the first time they met.

Carlos can tell it best:

"The first time I met Sharon's parents she had paid for a plane ticket for me from Washington, DC to Hartford. I had the flu that day, and that plus the prop plane ride gave me vertigo, so I was not in the best condition to make a good first impression. Sharon had cautioned me about her parents being a little old-fashioned, which I thought I could handle since I grew up surrounded by devout Catholics," he says.

"I was brought up to be polite, but I was never good at being deferential. I'm pretty much honest with everyone, and I was in no shape

to mask some of my surprise when I got to that house and met everyone. Two incidents stand out. Sharon had said that we probably would have to sleep in separate rooms. I thought this was just a little silly since we were already engaged and it was, after all, 1983. So when at the dinner table the subject came up, and Jack told me I would be sleeping in Tim's room, I made a humorously vulgar comment to the effect that Tim would be safe from me. The reaction I saw in Ginny, and Jack's faces were stonier than I could have imagined had I made the same remark to the most puritanical girlfriend's parents I had ever known.

"After dinner, I was shown the guest room in the basement (the one Sharon and I would not be permitted to stay in). In there was a grand piano. I sat down to play, setting down the can of beer I had been holding. Jack, moving so rapidly I could barely make it out, shot over to my side and placed a coaster under the can. I sensed that I had done something extraordinarily crass. I started to play and was immediately struck by how terrible it sounded: not just out of tune, but with the rust on the strings scratching at the very notes that struggled out of its deteriorated steel frame. I could not help myself; I asked Jack 'when was the last time this thing had gotten tuned?' I played a Scott Joplin rag, mumbling that it was something that would sound good on this piano. Most people I know with poor sounding pianos realize it and smile apologetically when someone plays them. Jack looked like I had killed his puppy."

Carlos goes on, "I don't think anything I said would have changed their opinion of me. There was no way I could impress. I was a couple of inches shorter than Sharon; I owned little more than a small car, against Sharon's house, land, and truck; I worked in a typing pool whereas Sharon had a high paying career. So I must have come off as a fortune hunter. They didn't come off well to me either. I was only in their house an hour before I sensed something upside down about their values. It wasn't just the piano, although the piano summed it up pretty well. It looked good, and they treated it like you would treat a prized possession, *with polish to protect the wood from decay and a hastily interposed coaster to protect it from me. But there was no substance behind it. It was like a Lincoln Continental sitting in a driveway, with brand new tires and a shiny coat of paint, covering up the fact that it needed an engine overhaul."*

"One other thing struck me. Sharon had gone on and on about how beautiful her mother was and even said that her sister was more attractive than her in some ways. I did not see this in either of them. Ginny was handsome enough for a 50-year-old, but I had a hard time seeing why Sharon would be intimidated by, or feel inferior to, either of them in the looks department. I told Sharon she should give herself more credit, and I wasn't just saying it to be nice."

We did muddle through having a sweet wedding in the yard at the dream house, with dozens of extended family members from both sides attending. Jack and Ginny were happy to show off their new property, and the wedding itself went well. I hoped that they would eventually get to know and like my husband and accept him as family.

I was leery of the birth control pill and was not as consistent with other methods as I ought to have been. We discovered that I was pregnant shortly before the wedding. Carlos and I kept it a secret from everyone until we returned to Dahlgren from our honeymoon. The first to be told were my parents. I was blind-sided by Ginny's reaction over the phone: she was furious with me. More than that, she insisted I had told my in-laws first. I had not, and told her so, but she didn't believe me.

When we told Carlos' family later that afternoon, they were excited for me and gave us nothing but warmth and support. I began to realize that my in-laws treated me much better than my own family did. A few weeks went by, and it came time for him to report to OCS. Carlos planned to stop over at my parent's house, a seven-hour drive from our home in Virginia (I still had the hardest time thinking about it as anything but my house) and about an hour from Newport. I hoped the dust had settled and perhaps, with some time and distance from the news of my unexpected pregnancy, they would begin to warm to the idea that the family was going to include Carlos and a baby soon.

They were polite at first when he arrived with his suitcase. But then Ginny became cold to Carlos, and Jack was worse. He took Carlos aside and berated him. He told him that it was cruel of him to make Ginny a grandmother. How do you think she feels about that? He demanded to know. Then he suggested the two of us were so screwed up that our marriage would fail and they would end up raising our baby themselves. Carlos relayed this to me just before he left my parents' house, whispering into the office telephone so no one could hear. I was hurt more deeply than I had ever been. I was alone, and I cried myself to sleep.

When I shared the story with a friend, she assured me that this was cruel behavior. I called Ginny and told her that if Jack didn't apologize, I would never speak to him again. He called a day later and apologized for upsetting me. A month later, I had a miscarriage at 13 weeks. I was hemorrhaging so badly that I thought I might die. I was rushed in an ambulance to the nearest military hospital, lying in a pool of my blood, and had an emergency abortion. My friends and colleagues were supportive and caring. My in-laws offered sympathy and told me that they had cried and prayed for us.

When I told my mother, she asked me if I had fallen. She provided no comfort. I later learned that she suggested to Jack and Tim that I had been irresponsible and lost the baby through some fault of my own. I realized I could never turn to my family for help. They had tried to poison my attitude toward my husband and had been cold and judgmental when I was suffering. I had lost a fetus at thirteen weeks. I was depressed, confused and anemic. My mother lost the trust of a twenty-six year-old daughter forever and didn't seem to notice.

Each evening for her last three decades, Ginny would lock the refrigerator and tell Eileen to go to bed. Eileen would frequently wait up until Ginny fell asleep on the couch with the Fox pundits babbling in the background. Then Eileen would pickpocket the refrigerator key and go to the kitchen. Sometimes Ginny woke up when she felt Eileen lift the key. Eileen once used scissors to carefully cut a slit in Ginny's jeans near the bottom of the pocket so that the key would slip out more easily. Sometimes Ginny woke up when she heard Eileen in the kitchen, or realized that Eileen had gotten a snack or went to the basement to do artwork. Ginny would furiously bully Eileen back to bed, shrieking and belittling her. Eileen would protest with a few words, slowly comply, and then pick at her skin or pull out her eyelashes. The Dream House was a nightmare for Eileen.

Cutting Ties

Carlos and I moved to San Diego California and began our lives together. We had a baby there, and after that, he got stationed in central New Jersey where we had second child. When the children were little, we drove the four-and-a-half hours to my parents' house to visit a few times each year. They acted happy to see me and their grandkids but made minimal effort to be supportive in any way. For example, one time when we were moving, we asked my parents for a

$2,000 loan so that we could make the down-payment on the house instead of waiting for the Navy to reimburse us for the cost of moving from California. Ginny lent me us the money as long as we paid the interest she would lose when she took the money out of an investment account. Carlos' parents once gave us $3,000 with no strings attached. They knew that we were struggling and they were unable to help us in ways they helped his brother and sisters as adults since we lived far away.

Ginny would occasionally send me envelopes full of newspaper or magazine articles she thought I would find interesting. She sent me copies of psychological reports on Eileen for me to read and discuss with her. The indication that she thought about me while she read the news was the closest thing to affection that I sensed from her during my adult life. In contrast, my in-laws lavished me with compliments and made it clear that they were happy and proud to have me in their family.

My mother had conditioned me to back down from arguments, first by using dismissive words, and then with violence, if I persisted. I had become passive in her presence; I became passive throughout my adulthood each time I visited her. There was no point in pushing an alternative point-of-view.

Jack even gave up and went along with her more and more as they aged. She stayed out of his business in a couple areas. He was free to play tennis without her approval or interference, and perform as a drummer and vocalist in jazz groups. He took care of the cars and mowed the one acre lot, skirting the flower and vegetable plots that were Ginny's exclusive domain.

The family was entitled to supportive services from the state of Connecticut to help them keep Eileen at home. It made sense for the state to help families care for disabled adults because institutionalizing them was far more costly. Ginny got help from a behavior specialist, who suggested locking the refrigerator and throwing away Eileen's meals and snacks if she dawdled, to encourage Eileen to comply in a more timely manner with Ginny's demands. This didn't seem to work, and the kitchen remained a constant battlefield until Ginny had her stroke.

Eileen continued to twitch, pick at her skin, and pull out her eyelashes. She stayed up at night and snuck to her arts and crafts desk in the basement. Her work became more repetitious. Eileen began creating the same designs over and over in various shades. She started doing odd things with tape and cotton taken from vitamin containers. She would make colored powders out of crayons or colored pencils, and then roll little puffs of cotton in the colored powder, wrap a strip of tape around the cotton puff, and then decorate the cellophane tape with more colors. She filled baskets and other decorative containers with these colored cotton puffs.

Ginny would befriend the state social workers sent to assist her in taking care of Eileen. She showed them around her beautiful home and gardens. The social workers received a mostly favorable impression of a lovely intelligent woman doing her best to provide a good home life for her disabled daughter.

Services from the state became more diversified as various private agencies began providing for the disabled population in exchange for state reimbursement. For a while, Eileen took part in art activities. She went to a studio where she had access to materials to make watercolor paintings of still-life and floral arrangements. Her work showed talent and skill. You would not judge these paintings to be anything but fine art created by a talented artist. Each year for 20 years, I would ask Ginny for one of Eileen's many pictures. Some of them were on display in the dream house, and piles of them collected dust in the basement.

I eventually got one for Christmas one year. It shows a small orange metal pail with a handle, filled with daisies. The stems and leaves are the usual green, but none of the petals are white; most of the flowers facing the viewer are shades of purple, while most flowers facing away are shades of dark yellow. I display this watercolor prominently in our home because it is beautiful and I am proud of Eileen's skill and persistence in creating art.

As the years passed, and I earned my credential as a school psychologist, our discussions became more and more one-sided. Ginny would talk, I would listen. If I suggested varying her ways of dealing with Eileen, I would get a long, droning, detailed and redundant description of all the things that she was doing. For any alternative proposed, Ginny could come up with a lecture on why the only possible solution was whatever she had already decided. She delivered rambling diatribes about how much paperwork was entailed doing anything with the new state services, how much other work she needed to do with her gardens, and for Tim's business that she and Jack had helped create.

Once I asked Tim why Mom was still doing the bookkeeping for his business. He told me that he hired a bookkeeper, but Mom would not turn the books over to her. Nothing changed very much in Ginny's routines or her appearance. Her hair stayed the same color, her makeup never varied; the basic bun was always firmly sprayed in place with AquaNet.

One thing did change Ginny's routine. In 1994, she became obsessed with the O.J. Simpson murder trial. My husband had just transferred to Cleveland, Ohio; our kids were aged eight and six, and we now had to endure a much longer drive to visit their grandparents in the summer. When we did visit, we found that the summer evening practice of having pre-dinner cocktails on the beach had stopped. Ginny didn't want to leave the television for fear of missing any new development about the murder trial.

After that, Ginny kept finding other news items she had to follow. When the Fox News channel began providing news tailored to older conservatives in 1996, she was hooked. She had remote speakers and then a TV screen installed in the kitchen. She ultimately stopped switching between shows and stations, and only tuned in to Fox News and a few other conservative news programs. Before Jack slipped into dementia, he would take the remote control and switch the channel to watch a movie or football game, but as he declined, the TV was tuned to Fox News almost all the time.

Ginny complained how tired she was with policing Eileen every night. Eileen had dark circles under eyes and often fell asleep at the sheltered workshop. The kind supervisors allowed Eileen to sleep there. I tried a few times to help Ginny break this cycle, but she would not budge. Tim offered a mini-fridge and microwave oven to make a kitchenette for Eileen, but this was refused.

By the time my own children were grown, it seems that Ginny and I had come to an impasse as well. I called every year on Mother's Day and on her birthday or Thanksgiving, whichever came first (her birthday was November 22). Ginny sent me birthday cards and called whenever a family member died. She always told me I was not expected to attend the funerals. Eventually, I stopped getting birthday cards and had to find out about deaths from my brother Tim.

As Jack slipped into confusion and Ginny became a droning one-way monologist so I made a deal with Tim. As I lived far away and had my own life I told him: since they were kind to him, put him through college, allowed him to live with them rent-free until he was over forty, and helped him start his business that the primary responsibility for their care, would fall on him as they aged and became feeble. Tim recognized that I had not been treated well by our parents, and agreed that he owed them more than I did. I asked him if he thought I needed to help in any way. He asked only that I be willing to listen to him if he felt the need to call me and complain about them. I assured him I was always available for that.

The End Is Near

Ginny refused to consider placing Eileen in a group home although Connecticut has terrific facilities where my sister would have been happier, healthier, and more functionally independent than at home. Ginny knew all about these group homes, being involved with an organization of parents of adult disabled people that advocated for programs and services. She was well aware of the quality of the facilities. I had worked in one such group home for over a year and assured her that the Clients experienced kindness and respect. They had comfortable, safe lives. Eileen would have been happier and encouraged to be more social in a group home.

Upon Ginny's death and the settling of the estate, it seems that in addition to a small Social Security check, which was enhanced because of the presence of a disabled household member and the $650 monthly disability check for my sister's care was what my mother was using to pay their bills. She had inherited hundreds of thousands of dollars from her parents and Aunt. She had many books and a keen interest in financial management, but she failed to structure investments in a way that would have left anything except the dream house and two other parcels of land with questionable value. The property taxes on the dream home were more than the Social security could cover along with food and utilities. The property taxes went unpaid with interest until most of the assets were gone. I felt sick thinking about it.

To the casual visitor, Ginny was a saint who loved her disabled daughter. Those who knew her saw her controlling my sister, keeping her under like a prisoner and refusing to allow her simple comforts like coffee with cream or the right to decide when to go to bed.

Although I was away serving in the Navy when the rest of the family relocated to the dream home, I was privy to the psychological reports and whatever perspective my mother shared when I called her. Ginny described Eileen regressing in her ability to function, and exhibiting OCD behaviors. In retrospect, another explanation of what happened suggests itself. At the old home in Tariffville, Ginny was usually busy running the family business and preparing for the big move. She and Jack spent months searching for the perfect property, planning the building and then relocating. I was no longer home to help. Eileen was left to her own devices, using the kitchen as she pleased without supervision.

When they moved, my parents become semi-retired; Ginny now had more time on her hands. My mother finally had her dream kitchen in her dream house and didn't want anyone making messes or getting in her way when she wanted to cook. She shooed Eileen out of the kitchen and Eileen became passive-aggressively slow about responding to Ginny's orders. Ginny raised her expectations and became more particular about Eileen's behavior. Eileen developed more OCD behaviors. This cycle would ratchet upwards until the day of the stroke.

Those of us who knew about the locked refrigerator that prevented Eileen from making herself a snack or putting cream in her instant coffee at night wondered what the big deal was. We wondered why Ginny lied to us, her other children, always saying that group home placement was impossible, that waiting lists were too long. I suggested that instead of fighting about bedtime, why didn't she let Eileen retire from the supervised work she did? That would end the nightly bedtime battles and the morning battles when Eileen didn't want to get out of bed and kept dawdling over breakfast.

Ginny insisted that if Eileen didn't go to the workshop, she herself would be unable to do her business of shopping and banking, always trapped at home, because if something went wrong, Eileen couldn't cope. What about teaching Eileen to use the phone and having Ginny's cell phone on speed dial? Impossible. How about letting Eileen have autonomy regarding eating and sleeping? This also met with stubborn resistance. It was hard to determine how many of Eileen's behavior problems were caused by Ginny's controlling behavior and how many were Eileen's symptoms.

As disabled adults go, Eileen was very easy to take care of. She preferred to keep to herself making art out of whatever she can find. She was eventually permitted to heat food in the microwave oven by herself, and would only need assistance in emergencies. Ginny refused to consider ending the constant struggle to make Eileen eat, sleep, and wake up so that she could be bused to a sheltered workshop where she took naps and accomplished very little.

Actually, Ginny was rarely out of the house for more than an hour, and there was state assistance for respite care to make it manageable for parents to keep disabled adults at home. Ginny was reluctant to use these services. She complained bitterly about how cumbersome the paperwork was. This made no sense at all. She had been the bookkeeper, administrator, and tax preparer for all of the family businesses. She refused to give up the bookkeeping she did for Tim's company even when Tim hired someone to take over. She of all people would have found bureaucratic paperwork at worst a minor annoyance.

Any conversation about changing her routine got diverted into a litany of her responsibilities. When I called on her birthday or Mother's day, I would spend nearly two hours mostly listening. It went something like this:

Me: "Happy Birthday Mom, how's it going?"

Ginny: "This weather is ridiculous; it's been so cold lately. The yard is a mess, because the water pipe was replaced and they dug a long strip through the yard, and now it is all muddy because of the rain, and it's too late to plant grass, and the driveway is all torn up, and there are rocks and clay all over the garden and your father is no help because he can't follow directions. How are you?"

Me: "Oh pretty good. I've been doing some work with a nonprofit that helps adults with learning disabilities and…"

Ginny: "I had to take your father to the VA again to get his medication adjusted it's such a long drive, and he can't remember anything anymore, so I have to go in there with him and talk to the doctor because he doesn't remember anymore what happened last week and now I have to watch him all the time and what with the yard and Eileen and the rain, it's a constant mess out there and…"

Me: "Have you thought about getting some help?"

Ginny: "Eileen's social worker came by the other day, and we had a long talk, you would like her she's very nice, so anyway the paperwork is ridiculous. Every time somebody takes her out I have to fill out a form so they can get paid. It's gotten so bad nobody wants to do this kind of work anymore because of the paperwork. Everything the state does is a mess, they make it too hard to do anything, and I have all this other stuff to do with your father and Tim's business, and the weather has been just awful, and the yard is a mess. It's going to take a lot of work to clean up the mess they made when they replaced the water pipe…"

Me: "Maybe Eileen would enjoy a week of respite care while you got caught up with things?"

Ginny: "I heard on the news about mass murder, what is this world coming to? Why are people killing everyone? And this problem is all over and getting worse and worse all the time…"

Me: "Actually, statistically, the crime rate has never been lower. You really should turn off the TV and listen to music or something else instead-"

Ginny: "Oh, I only watch a few shows and have it on in the background while I do other things. Did you hear about what they are doing in downtown New London they are building some kind of pier that's supposed to be good for the economy and they are wasting millions of dollars of tax money because they got a big federal grant and they're building this monstrosity that's going to cost a lot and if they ever finish it probably won't make any difference for the economy because nobody wants to go there because of the crime..."

Me: "The last time I was in New London, it seemed kind of cute. It looks like there are some new shops and restaurants. It looks like they cleaned the place up," I replied.

Ginny: "Oh, what's this world coming to? There is so much crime and people doing horrible things. I read in the paper about a man who killed his wife and sent her corpse through the wood chipper. They found bits of her bones all over the place...Why do people do things like that?

Me: "You're just more aware of the terrible things that happen because you have cable news on all the time and read all the newspapers. You know what they say if it bleeds it leads-"

Ginny: "Well, there's still something not right with the water pipe. They're going to be tearing it up again and making a big mess that's going waste a lot of money...How is your family doing?"

Me: Fine, Carlos got promoted and...

(it usually continued in this fashion for ninety more minutes)

Ginny: "Well thanks for calling; I don't want to take all of your money."

Me: "It's OK. It's a cell phone, and I have unlimited long distance with my plan-"

Ginny: "Well, thanks for calling, I have so many things to do now, and I'm sure you do too. How's the weather where you are?"

Me: "It's getting cold, but we had a lovely Fall, I kept getting tomatoes until October this year and canned some soups and sauces."

Ginny: "I don't know how you find the time to do canning, doesn't it take all day?"

Me: "No, not really."

Ginny: "Well, thanks for calling; I hope you don't get clobbered too badly this winter with the snow and all."

Me: "It's Ok, it snows every winter, and we're prepared for it."

Ginny: "OK, well goodbye."

Me: "Goodbye and Happy birthday."

My Last Visit

I visited the dream house in June 2017. It was the last time I would see my parents alive. I was sixty years-old, and Ginny was eighty-four. Jack was still alive but confused most of the time. He was able to recognize me and over dinner one night suddenly looked at me and said, "I miss you, Sharon." Staying at the dream house was difficult. The Foxnews Cable channel was on all the time and the volume had gone up as Ginny's hearing weakened. She was telling me about the state of my Father and sister with the TV blaring.

"I can't listen to you with that in the background, and I want to know what you are telling me," I said. "Ok, well I'll turn it down a little," she said as she adjusted the volume, "I don't want to miss anything."

She let me prune her blueberry bushes. I had become a Master Gardener and told her that my own blueberry bushes were thriving under my care. She brought her tools out to the blueberry patch and watched while I showed her how I would cut out the old branches and remove any unwanted weed sprouts. This was a breakthrough in our relationship in that she trusted my knowledge and expertise. All of my adult life, she treated my ideas, suggestions, and opinions as inferior or even delusional. She didn't trust me to help her with anything unless she supervised or gave me annoyingly explicit instructions.

Another surprise was when I suggested that she consider what would happen to my father and sister if something happened to her. What if she became unable to keep taking care of everything? She actually paused for a few seconds instead of immediately interrupting me. Then she changed the subject.

I was still working as a school psychologist when Ginny died. Because I have a copy of the DSM-V in my office, a relative asked me to send information about Obsessive-Compulsive Personality Disorder (OCPD). This was not my area of professional expertise although I was familiar with personality disorders from graduate school teaching general psychology classes. I was familiar with other personality disorders. All people with personality disorders lack insight into their own behavior. They tend to do the same dysfunctional behaviors over and over and blame others for their misfortune.

Before scanning and sending the pages containing the diagnostic features of OCPD, I read them; all I saw were descriptions of my mother: she was controlling, things had to be done her way, and she had no flexibility about how things should be done. She refused to consider the opinions of others. She was often unable to make decisions that required changes in routines. She could not trust anyone to help her with any tasks that she believed had to be done the way she had been doing them. She was so busy taking care of things by herself that she had no time for travel, recreation or any leisure activities. Her hobby of gardening became a burdensome task that overwhelmed her. When offered help she insisted on supervising or micromanaging to such a degree that it caused those closest to her to give up trying to help.

Ginny did not express affection or appreciation to those close to her. She was not comfortable with others demonstrating emotions. Although she demonstrated a high level of intelligence in her knowledge base and ability to understand and retain information, she lacked insight about her own situation. She could not understand how she made her own life more difficult by refusing to consider changing her routines. She complained bitterly about how busy she was to the very people who tried to offer suggestions and assistance in making her life better.

The house was full of collectible items that Ginny believed were valuable. Although taxes and bills went unpaid, she never considered selling any of the hundreds of items she had collected from her ancestors. Most of these items were in less than perfect condition and not worth nearly the value she placed on these items. She kept the common areas of the home neat, but the basement and storage areas were packed with hundreds of potentially useful things in quantities that were absurd. Hundreds of coffee cans, cheap vases, discolored silverware, upholstery fabric, buttons, thread, and old clothes packed the recesses of the house. She was unable to let go of things that might be useful or valuable to a degree that most items she might have wanted or needed was buried under piles of other potentially useful things.

Ginny may have been suffering from a disorder that blinded her to her own predicaments and isolated her from those who could help. Some suggest that she may have been on the Autism spectrum, but without observing her as a child, this diagnosis would not be possible. She ruminated and obsessed over the same issues without being able to adjust to changes in circumstances. She was unable or unwilling to consider points of view that diverged from hers.

An online description of OCPD is available; see DSM-4
@

https://www.healthline.com/health/obsessive-compulsive-personality-disorder#symptoms

I was under the impression that Ginny was good with money and so were a lot of other people. When I was in grade school, she took over the bookkeeping for the family business, taking advice from the man who lived across the street, Mr. Dematae. He probably was doing their business taxes at that point, or maybe he was just a helpful neighbor. In any case, he taught her to arrange the system of journals, ledgers, and retained documents, and showed her how to itemize expenses so that their tax burden was as low as possible.

Ginny was proud of this role she played. Each April she spent two weeks sitting in the sunroom with an adding machine and stacks of files, making sure that the absolute minimum (or better yet, zero) taxes were paid on their business income.

She continued to keep up with the rules by reading trade magazines and books. She liked discussing her responsibilities and expertise. Once, Personnel Search Associates was subjected to a tax audit. She and Jack had to spend time at the IRS defending the books. Ginny was able to provide documentation and legal reasons for every question they had.

She was supremely irritated at the time required to answer those questions, later ranting that the IRS should have paid her for the time that she believed was wasted for no good reason. She often referenced this experience as an example of how government know-nothings rob hard working business people of what is rightfully theirs.

There was little nuance in her view that the government was inefficient and wasteful. She believed that government workers had cushy jobs that required little effort and provided far too much compensation. She thought they did not deserve the lifestyles they led, financed by taxes paid by much more deserving business people.

Ginny was good at giving the impression that she knew far more than most other people. I don't know if she believed that she was smarter than anyone else or worried that she wasn't as sharp as people gave her credit for. In arguments, Ginny insisted she was right and often cited her excellent memory to bolster her views. But she did not come off as confrontational; she was able to keep quiet and listen. This, added to her good looks, gave her an air of mystery and perhaps made it easy to assume she was very knowledgeable.

She did the books for the headhunting agency and the real estate business. Business had slowed down after they moved to Waterford. But then Tim began selling renovated outboard motors out of the garage. Jack and Ginny urged him to set up shop in a small rental property they had obtained nearby. Encouraging Tim to expand, Jack ran errands and worked on various projects as Tim got more customers.

It seemed like a good deal to Tim; he had both his parents working for him for free as well as providing him with a beautiful place to live with cooking and laundry services. Ginny soon offered to take over the bookkeeping.

Tim made the mistake of trusting his mother's expertise as a bookkeeper. Ginny was secretive about what was going on with Tim's finances, but he was too busy with operations and marketing to worry about what she was doing. At one point he took over the management of a nearby marina and added several employees. Tim rarely took time off and worked long hours. He had little time for a social life and never married or started a family.

It became apparent during her last years of life that the family and business finances were not doing well underneath the surface. Although Ginny inherited a significant amount of money and real estate, and they had made a lot of money wheeling and dealing real estate, investing and planning for the future were not things Ginny was good at. She had many finance and accounting books she had studied. She may have believed she had inherited a knack for investing. Albert lived very simply, invested very carefully and left nearly a million dollars worth of assets to Ginny and her brother when he and Lily passed away in 2004.

Ginny inherited the house that her grandparents lived in, having assisted her Aunt Lena as she aged. She inherited half of her Parents' estate. I assumed she had invested those assets. Other than the impressive home, they lived meagerly. They never traveled or ate out. They did all their own home maintenance and repairs. Jack fixed up wrecked cars he purchased at insurance auctions and kept them running for decades.

But all was not well in Ginny's financial management. It turns out she didn't regularly pay property taxes on the dream home. And at some point, she stopped paying payroll taxes for Tim's business. Jack died, and Ginny a few weeks later. Tim emailed the will to Dan and me. Eileen would get nothing because anything left to her would be absorbed by the state of Connecticut when she finally went to a group home. So the estate was to be split three ways between Dan, Tim and me.

I flew to Connecticut for the week of Thanksgiving to help Tim deal with Eileen's situation and the dream house. He had already been working with an art and antique appraiser to help dispose of all the valuables collected from so many relatives and properties. There were a significant number of valuable pieces, but many of them were not in the kind of pristine condition that would attract top dollar; a tiny chip on a vintage ceramic piece would reduce its value from $100 at an antique store to a few dollars at a yard sale.

Tim and I held a few estate sales and moved truckloads of items passed over by the appraiser as not particularly valuable. We made enough money to keep the house utilities and property taxes paid for a little while. The money that came in from the valuable arts and antiques would mostly go to lawyers and estate expenses. Ginny was the curate of a museum of mostly junk, with a few valuable items mixed in.

About four years earlier, the property taxes had gone unpaid for nearly a decade. The county of New London would have been threatening to auction off the house. Ginny sold a lot for $350,000 to pay the taxes and interest. (She had refused a purchase offer of $900,000 on that same lot before the real estate bubble burst in 2008.) The 18% interest portion of the delinquent tax bill was almost two-thirds of the total due. That's $228,000 that would not have been charged if the taxes had only been paid on time. The property tax penalties would have been enough to buy college for all of Jack and Ginny's grandchildren. The missed profits on that lot could have paid their property taxes on time, traveled and had household help. There was nothing left. The only income Ginny had was Jack's social security and the $650 in disability benefits for Eileen. She had not invested wisely, converted any of the financial windfalls into ready cash annuities, or turned the hundreds of thousands inherited and earned over the years into anything. She had a dream house, a few valuable things, and not much else.

It seems that her oft-repeated lie about there being no place for Eileen in a group home was done to protect the income Eileen's residency provided. Eileen was used as a cash cow to keep Ginny in her dream home and pay the cable bill that kept her beloved Fox News on 24/7.

Eileen now lives in a group home. She goes to bed at a reasonable time and wakes up early to make herself breakfast. The staff at the group home finds her appealing. They are patient and considerate of her needs and desires. Eileen is cooperative and claims to be happy with the arrangement. Her obsessive-compulsive behaviors have diminished, and the circles under her eyes are not as deep. Tim takes Eileen out to restaurants, stores, and museums regularly.

DAFFODIL

I love my spring flower

it has honey inside

Yellow color like a house I know

Nothing else as yellow

As my spring colored daffodil.

-Eileen

Sharing a bedroom with a sister who giggled for no apparent reason, talked nonsense, and created artwork obsessively inspired me to study psychology. It took me years to get my Bachelor's degree (BA) and more than twenty years to get my Masters (MA) in Psychology as well as certification as a school psychologist.

My first attempt at graduate school in the 1970s, I had problems dealing with the classes. I wasn't comfortable labeling people with things like latent homosexuality because they saw furry blankets in the Rorschach tests. Homosexuality was still considered a disease back then and old-school psychologist worried that the "latent" (hidden, unconscious, or inactive) condition could cause all kinds of problems. I couldn't go along with things that didn't make sense to me. At the time it was determined that I just wasn't ready for graduate school. So I did a few other things until I was ready.

When I finally started my becoming a psychologist in the 1990s, things had changed since I had first attempted graduate school. Since the 70s, some disorders disappeared or were changed, and others were added by the American Psychiatric Association (APA). Some definitions and names of psychological and psychiatric conditions were changed. The APA had new speculations regarding the causality of some mental illnesses. The program I enrolled in allowed students to express uncertainty and ask questions about things that nobody knew for sure instead of acting as if we knew it all.

I specialized in school psychology because it made the most sense to me. I had worked as a special education teacher for a few years during my detour. This meant mostly giving a lot of tests, mostly IQ and academic achievement tests; also behavior checklists to determine if people have Attention Deficit Hyperactivity Disorder. (ADHD) There are other checklists to identify Autism Spectrum Disorder. (ASD) In the last couple of decades, I've given over a million tests. The more people I work with, and all-the-while continue to study psychology, the more questions I have.

When IQ (Intelligence Quotient) tests first came out, the score was based on a mathematical formula where the chronological age is divided by the mental age and multiplied by100. The mental age was determined by testing someone's skills on various tasks, and comparing that score to a norm based on the average test scores of people at different ages. The formula resulted in a score whereby test takers who performed at an average level for their age achieved an IQ of 100, those who scored like those who were older achieved higher IQ scores and those who tested similarly to younger people achieved lower IQ scores.

This formula is not in use anymore and hasn't been for decades. We still call them IQ tests, but they are no longer based on the Intelligence quotient formula. What we use now is a deviation score based on how far away from average a score falls on a bell curve of measured human characteristics. One's IQ score should really be called an *intelligence deviation number*. The statistical technique is also used to help determine if a person qualifies as being Depressed, Learning Disabled, Autistic on the Autism Spectrum, or suffering from ADHD.

The first IQ tests were given to children determine why some of them failed in school. If they had low IQs, they were labeled as morons, idiots, or imbeciles (the clinical terms in use in the early 20th Century) for IQs ranging from 0 to 25, 26 to 50, and 51 to 70, respectively. Those terms were later changed to Profoundly, Severely and Trainable Mentally Retarded (PMR, SMR, and TMR). Another category was added for those with a low IQ who could learn to read and do math at a fundamental level. They were called Educable Mentally Retarded (EMR). Terms used by the psychology profession to describe levels of intelligence quickly entered the common language, or vernacular, as insults. I remember back in elementary school being asked sarcastically if I was "Mental". If I knew then what I know now, I may have said, "Yes!—and physical too!" I would probably have gotten more ridicule had I replied in such a manner.

The profession tried to keep ahead of this trend by referring to psychological conditions based on the gradations of limited intelligence by their acronyms: EMR, TMR, and so on. After the term 'retarded' became a common insult, the limited intelligence description was changed to Developmentally Delayed or Developmentally Disabled (DD), then briefly back to Mentally Retarded, (MR) to avoid having people believe that this condition would be outgrown. The R-word, i.e. retarded, was still problematic; so in the 1990s, it was changed to Cognitively Disabled (CD) and only in the last few years to the most recent term Intellectually Disabled (ID). This sounds more dignified, and serves for the time being.

When I finally completed my graduate degree, it was a Master of Arts or MA.in Psychology. I think the fact that a psychology degree is considered an art rather than a science degree is unfortunate but true. Psychology is slowly transforming into a more scientific field, but it continues to carry the baggage of refuted ideas and flawed theories. I can

232

call myself a psychologist because of the program of study I completed, as well as meeting the Ohio Department of Education standards for School Psychology—this required passing a test and performing a one-year internship after finishing my degree.

After working as a school psychologist for three years, I took another test and acquired a professional license to practice school psychology in the state of Ohio. Now I can list SP after my name to denote that license. If I move to another state, or stop paying a biannual fee, I will lose those letters. Although I considered going for a PhD degree a few times in my life, my primary goal was to be able to work with people and use my knowledge to help them. I have been able to accomplish that for the most part.

I had worked with children in the late 70s; I encountered kids with various classifications. Most schools had designations for Emotionally Disturbed (ED), Developmentally Delayed (DD) and Learning Disabled (LD). These terms varied from state to state. Educational facilities used different terminology than the medical and psychiatric professions used. Each state in the United States had their own variations on these labels until 1990 when new federal laws forced more consistent rights for disabled students and procedures for dealing with them. Children who previously were ED were changed to SBH (Severe Behavior Handicapped), and then went back to being ED in this century. The LD kids became SLD (Specific Learning Disabled). The Autism Spectrum Disorder has only been used in schools for the last ten years.

There is no new "epidemic" of ASD. These conditions have always existed, but only became known about when the DSM III, and subsequent editions, listed them. The surge in children with this label occurred as a result of getting the label from a local pediatrician or psychologist rather than traveling to Vienna or Baltimore to meet with one of the two experts who had some clinically-based observations and the beginnings of treatment protocols.

When I worked at Capitol Region Education Center (CREC) in the late 1970s, a psychologist developed behavioral treatment plans all of the children. We childcare workers were charged with awarding those kids points for avoiding problem behaviors as well as participating appropriately. If they earned most of their points, they could purchase privileges and coupons to spend in a little store. They could go on outings, go swimming, or watch movies. If they failed to earn points, they spent their evenings in a room with no entertainment. Behavior modification was all the rage and the behaviorist school didn't put much stock in labels for psychological problems. They focused only on observable and measurable behavior.

As a lowly childcare worker and lifeguard, I didn't have access to the student records that contained descriptions of their mental health conditions. I asked the full-time workers about some of the students. Some were Juvenile Delinquents (JD), some were MR, and some were ED. I liked to know the classifications and the histories of the kids so I could understand them better. There were some kids at CREC with quirky behaviors.

Some of the kids would get points for avoiding odd behaviors like perseverating (repetitive, ritualistic behavior) or self-stimulating. There was a girl, Charlene, who wasn't supposed to perseverate. She liked to say certain words over and over. One of her favorite words was "chisel" for some unknown reason. She would ask for her point card and want to know if she had lost any points for perseverating. She often lost points because she kept asking the same question in different forms. "I'm not perseverating, am I? You don't think I'm perseverating do you? I don't think I perseverated too much, do you?" If teacher suggested that Charlene was perseverating, she became upset and loudly protested that she, "DID NOT perseverate too much".

The boy who wasn't supposed to self-stimulate liked to pull on his lip, or poke at the palm of his hand with his finger. He tried to do it furtively, but alert teachers or childcare workers often saw him and told that he was not going to earn his points because of self stimulating. He looked sad when he lost his points. I tended to overlook these behaviors because they seemed to be soothing to the kids, and I believed it was cruel to prevent them from doing things that only made them look odd to others but didn't hurt anyone. I was uncomfortable with the focus back then of trying to get these kids to look and act as normal as possible without bothering to understand what made them act different in the first place.

I believe that growing up with an odd sister made me more tolerant of odd behavior than most. We still had no specific diagnosis for my sister Eileen, but some of the children at CREC reminded me of her. Some of the children walked awkwardly, giggled at the sounds of certain words or made unusual gestures, and facial expressions. They had these things in common with my sister. I asked some of the staff members who had access to the records how these kids were classified.

"That one is an FLK and that one is a GOK" I was told by someone who had been working with these kids for a longer time than me. I asked, "What does that mean?

"FLK means *Funny Looking Kid* and GOK means *God Only Knows*." They tossed these acronyms around in jest. It seems natural to find humor in a system where labels and acronyms didn't help us understand very much. While the diagnosis of Autism, Asperger's, and the Autism Spectrum was not commonly known until 1980. It seems that FLK and GOK were some of the terms used to describe those children who in later years would be likely to be classified as having what we now call Autisms Spectrum Disorders. Today, there are people on the Autism Spectrum who refer to some of us as NT or Neurotypical. This reminds me of a man who worked as an advocate for disabled people while having a fairly obvious problem with Cerebral Palsy. In response to be called a CP rather than *a person with CP*, he took to calling other people 'AB' (for Able-Bodied). It must be tiring to be labeled with a term that only describes what makes one different from most other people. We need to be reminded that each person is more than the thing that makes them different. I have been fortunate to have avoided being identified with any particular clinical label except for a short time when I gave birth in 1986.

I tried to have a home birth but my blood pressure was so high that I was sent to the hospital where I could be treated with an IV drip while I pushed out an 8 and 1/2 pound baby. Because of the IV drip I was sent to the complication ward to recover with all the women who had C-sections (Cesarean Sections). The nurses kept visiting me to check on my stitches and discussed with each other that there were no stitches on my belly. I overheard them explain this to each other by saying, "She's a Vadge." They labeled me a vadge (short for "vagina") because of how my baby exited my body. I was the only woman called a "Vadge" in the complications ward. It was written on the Chart that hung on a clipboard attached to my bed. I struggled with the label that reduced me to part of the name of the body part that I pushed a baby through. Fortunately for me, this was a temporary epithet.

It is tough—and more often than not, stigmatizing—to go through life being referred to by the thing that makes one different. People shouldn't be reduced to labels that only describe part of what or who they might be. What I have learned over the years working with disabled people is that most of them are only slightly different from those of us who are considered normal. The rules may change any time and some of us who are considered normal at his point in time may have a clinical label sometime in the future. It wasn't that long ago that most people were illiterate so it wouldn't matter if you were LD or learning disabled. When labels help us understand and find ways to help people they can be a good thing. The important, and challenging, part of labeling is to see the label is a means of understanding the individual who has that label. Far better to not use the label to define the person as an object or thing that the label seeks to somehow explain. If one has known one person with a particular label, one only knows that one person, and possibly solely by that label. The others who share the same label have a few things in common, but they are all unique individuals as well.

Disabled kids were integrated into the Least Restrictive Environment in 1973, sometimes referred to as the LRE law or FAPE (Free Appropriate Public Education). That meant that rather than being shut away in special schools were they were not seen by the majority of Able-Bodied and Neurotypical children. Now, all kinds of kids go to school together. This normalizes things for the kids with disabilities and provides some perspective for their Neurotypical and

Able-Bodied peers those previous generations might have missed out on.

I remember one time when a florescent light in my home flickered so much I said that I felt like that thing was going to give me a seizure. My fifth grade son said, "You mean like this?" Then he did a perfect demonstration of a seizure. I asked him how he knew about seizures and he explained that one of his classmates had them occasionally. It was not a big deal to him. His classmates all knew that when this happened they needed to move the furniture away from this boy, and when it was over they give him time to recover. This was reported as matter-factly as a lesson about the Lewis and Clark expedition might have been.

With all the problems in the world today, I have hope for the future when I see how kids understand and accept each other so much better than previous generations. Inclusion and integration benefits everyone, although there are many challenges to making it work, each generation seems to gets better at it.

The field of psychology is not based on a solid foundation of science and facts. As society changes, the areas of neurology, biology, and medicine make breakthroughs, psychology adapts in fits and starts to new knowledge, while old ideas and theories refuse to die. In graduate school, you can discuss the foundations and history of various methods of assessment and the reasons to label people with psychological conditions. In 1851, in the Antebellum South, it was believed slaves who wanted to run away suffered from a concocted condition called *Drapetomania*. Freud thought women who wanted to be in charge of their own lives suffered from *penis envy*. The ancient Greeks used the term *hysteria* to describe what happened to women when their uteri moved about to various places in their bodies. We eventually move away from old ideas, and eventually, social changes happen. Sometimes it helps to look at things from a historical perspective to see progress.

It's alright to be uncomfortable around people who don't seem to operate normally. Our fear of those who are different than what we are used to may have an evolutionary component that makes us reflexively wary of the unfamiliar. It's reasonable to grieve if you have a family member with limited potential; it is natural to mourn for the loss of hopes and dreams of typical life developments. It's natural to worry about how families or society can take care of those with exceptional needs. Sometimes it's easier to focus too much on what is wrong with people than what is right with them.

I often work with children in school, to find out what it is about them that made their teachers or parents refer them for a Multi-Factored Evaluation (MFE). I spend hours analyzing test results and writing reports explaining how these children need Individual Education Plans (IEPS) because they have a "handicapping condition" under the *Individuals with Disabilities in Education Act* (IDEA); Pub.L 101-476, 104 Stat. 1142 (which was preceded by the *Education for All Handicapped Children Act* (EAHCA or EHA) of 1975; Pub.L. 94-142).

I sometimes need to recover from the negative focus of this work. I look at kids while they play and see my little clients doing what children do naturally. I feel relieved that in spite of having various brain problems, they usually can laugh, play, and socialize as well or nearly as well as their Neurotypical and Able-Bodied peers. Kindergarten rooms are the best places to find hope. A room full of small people who can't read, write, or earn money, but are happily learning to follow directions and do things with crayons will do wonders for my sense that all people have value and the capacity for joy.

I have had some amazing colleagues over the decades that can look beyond the labels and disabilities so they can see the amazing things some of the most disabled people can do. I find it interesting that people who will tell you how smart their dog or cat is and will ask me if it's depressing to work with disabled people, to which I reply, "Definitely not."

I went to college to find answers to my questions about my sister, and try to understand human nature. I didn't find all that I was looking for, but I did find a career helping students get some of the support they needed in school. From outside the ivory tower of research and knowledge, psychology seems to hold answers and explanations that are clear and comprehensive. The inside story is a more messy. The names of contemporary techniques and theories are similar to an alphabet soup of random pieces of knowledge, mixed in with chunks of outdated theories and pseudoscience. There are some real pieces of substance floating in this broth, and some hope and some help for people. Someday we may have better ways to understand and help people with disabilities, mental illness, and psychological problems—or whatever terms become popular ways to describe how brains fail to conform to expectations. When understanding fails, compassion can fill the void; and, compassion is one of the rare things of which I *am* sure.

240

Questions for the Reader

If you have Autism in your family or are familiar with families dealing with autism, how does the Hogan Family compare to families you have known?

Do you or someone you know have a sibling who is disabled or health-impaired? If so, does Sharon's experience seem similar to other siblings?

Siblings of those with medical or psychiatric problems are often inspired by these experiences to enter the helping professions. What reactions by siblings of ill or disabled people have you seen?

The Baby boom included children born between 1946 and 1964. How do the experiences of the Hogan family compare to others of that era?

Do Sharon's parents seem typical or unique for their era compared to other parents of the baby boom generation?

How did you react to the account of the history of Autism research described in the book?

Families respond to serious mental or physical health problems in unique ways. Does the Hogan family seem similar to or different from other families you have seen?

Mother-daughter relationships are often complex and difficult. How does the relationship described by Sharon with her mother compare with mother-daughter relationships you have known?

Mother's often have responsibility and control over many aspects of families. How does Ginny's family management compare with mothers you have known?

What do you think about how do the themes of feminism and political differences between generations play out for the Hogan family?

Suggested Readings

American Psychiatric Association. *Diagnostic and Statistical Manual of Mental Disorders, Fifth Edition: DSM-5.* Arlington: American Psychiatric Publishing, 2013.

Baron-Cohen, Simon. *Mind Blindness An Essay on Autism and Theory of Mind.* Cambridge MA, London: The MIT Press, 1995.

Grandin, Temple. *The Way I See It: A Personal Look at Autism and Asperger's.* Arlington TX: Future Horizons, 2014.

Grandin, Temple. *Thinking in Pictures: My Life With Autism.* New York: Vantage Books, 2006.

Grinker, Richard. *Unstrange Minds Remapping the World of Autism.* New York: Perseus Books Group, 2007.

Higashiday, Naoki, and Yoshiida, Ka. *The Reason I Jump the Inner Voice of a Thirteen-Year-Old Boy with Autism.* Translated by David Mitchell. New York: Random House ©2007, 2013 (1st English Edition).

Notbohm, Ellen. *Ten Things Every Child with Autism Wishes You Knew.* Arlington TX: Future Horizons, 2005.

Peete, Elizabeth, Peete R.J., Robinson, Holly, and Ryan, Elizabeth. *Same but Different: Teen life on the Autism Express.* New York: Scholastic Press, 2016.

Robinson, John Elder. *Be Different Adventures of a Free-range Aspergian.* New York: Broadway Paper Backs, 2011.

Robinson, John Elder. *Look Me in the Eye.* New York: Crown Publishing, 2007.

Sacks, Oliver. *An Anthropologist on Mars: Seven Paradoxical Tales.* New York: Vantage Books, 1995.

Acknowledgements

A rich mixture of history, community, ancestry and chance dropped me in a time and place that inspired me to seek meaning and purpose. I am grateful for the inspiration of heroes as well as villains; good fortunes and bad. (Some of the names have been changed to protect those who might not appreciate how they were portrayed.) All the forces and individuals that gave me the life and opportunities I have are far too numerous to mention. A few deserve thanks for making this book possible:

First I'd like to thank my husband, who has been my constant companion for thirty-five years and my first reader. His encouragement and suggestions helped me form a scattered collection of memories and ideas into a coherent narrative.

The editor who I met by chance at the library, Wm. Joseph Robertson, has helped pull this project across the finish line. His knowledge, patience, and attention to detail showed me, as a first-time author, what a book needs to be ready for publication.

Lisa Griffis is the graphic artist who designed the cover and organized the illustrations. Her professionalism, encouragement, and spirit helped covert my vague ideas into visual reality.

All the teachers, researchers, professors, and practitioners in the mental health field who slowly moved us out of the dark ages deserve more thanks than they ever get.

About the Author

Sharon Hogan is a licensed School Psychologist who lives in the Cleveland area (Lakewood, Ohio). She has been a United States Naval officer, a Special Education teacher, and Summer Camp Counselor and Director.

She has been an Adjunct Professor teaching Human Development and Educational Psychology classes as well as general psychology for fifteen years.

She helps people with learning disabilities and other issues in private practice, and in area schools. She lives in a century-old home near Lake Erie with her husband of thirty-five years where she is compelled to grow flowers and food in her yard.

If you enjoyed this book, please write a review on Amazon.

You can find links to purchase this book in kindle or print editions on amazon.com

Read blogs and view more pictures by visiting the website Sharon shares with her husband: www.cliftonsummit.com

You can order a signed print copy by contacting the Author

Sharon is available to speak to groups on a number of themes included in this book.

If you want to arrange a talk, or just want to correspond with Sharon, please do!

fairychildsister@gmail.com

Made in the USA
Lexington, KY
24 June 2019